ML 670

ACPL ITEM
DISCARDED

3 1833 00 33 5873

332.414
In32
Inflation: causes, consequents,
and control

SO-BWM-530

DO NOT REMOVE
CARDS FROM POCKET

ALLEN COUNTY PUBLIC LIBRARY

FORT WAYNE, INDIANA 46802

You may return this book to any agency, branch,
or bookmobile of the Allen County Public Library

DEMCO

INFLATION

Dedicated to

Arthur Sullivan Gale, Jr.

and

Harriet Cross Gale

loving parents

INFLATION

Causes, Consequents, and Control

Edited by

William A. Gale

*Bell Telephone
Laboratories, Inc.*

Oelgeschlager, Gunn & Hain, Publishers, Inc.
Cambridge, Massachusetts

ALLEN COUNTY PUBLIC LIBRARY
EORT WAYNE, INDIANA

Copyright © 1981 Bell Telephone Laboratories, Incorporated. All rights reserved. No part of this publication may be reproduced, stored in a retrieval system, or transmitted in any form or by any means, electronic mechanical photocopy, recording or otherwise, without the prior written consent of the publisher.

Internation Standard Book Number: 0-89946-118-2

Library of Congress Catalog Card Number: 81-9612

Printed in West Germany

Library of Congress Cataloging in Publication Data
Main entry under title:

Inflation: causes, consequents, and control.

　　Includes bibliographical references and index.
　　Contents: Introduction / William A. Gale — Perceptions (or misperceptions) of inflation / John A. Carlson — How well can we measure price changes? / William A. Gale — [etc.]
　　1. Inflation (Finance)—Addresses, essays, lectures. 2. Inflation (Finance)—United States—Addresses, essays, lectures. I. Gale, William A.
HG229.I4513　　　　　332.4'1'0973　　　　81-9612
ISBN 0-89946-118-2　　　　　　　　　　　　AACR2

Contents

2161931

List of Figures   vii

List of Tables   ix

Preface   xi

Chapter 1   Introduction   1
             William A. Gale

Chapter 2   Perceptions (or Misperceptions) of Inflation
             John A. Carlson
             Introduction   13
             2. Recent U. S. Experience   15
             3. Relative Price Changes and Perceived Inflation   20
             4. Survey Evidence of Expected Inflation   24
             5. Statistical Approaches to Inflation Expectations   31
             6. Survey Evidence vs. Time-Series Forecasts   37
             7. Concluding Remarks   44

Chapter 3   How Well Can We Measure Price Changes?
             William A. Gale
             Introduction   51
             2. Criterion   53
             3. Discussion of Errors   59
             4. Differences Not Quantified   85
             5. Correction for Bias   85
             6. Comparison of Effects   87
             7. Summary   97
             Appendix A   97
             Appendix B   109

Chapter 4 The International Economy as a Source of and
           Restraint on U.S. Inflation
           Michael R. Darby
           Introduction   115
           2. Proximate Determinants of the Inflation Rate   116
           3. Determinants of Nominal Money Supply Growth   119
           4. Determinants of Real Money Demand Growth   123
           5. Conclusions and Summary   130

Chapter 5 Why the Great Inflation Has Been a Catastrophe
           Paul Evans
           Introduction   133
           2. Inflation and Relative Prices   134
           3. The Tax Laws   135
           4. A Theoretical Analysis of the Effects of a Rising
              Marginal Tax Rate   138
           5. Simulating the Effects of a Rising Marginal
              Tax Rate   143
           6. Conclusions   153
           Appendix A   153
           Appendix B   158
           Appendix C   162

Chapter 6 Some Perspectives on Controlling U. S. Inflation
           Michael Bazdarich
           Introduction   167
           2. Inflation, the Money Supply, and Cost-Push   169
           3. The Granger Causality Technique   172
           4. Results of the Tests   177
           5. Some Episodes of Inflation   182
           6. Conclusion--Controlling Inflation

Index   193

About the Editor   197

List of Figures

Chapter 1

1.1   Hundred-year Overview of U.S. Inflation   6
1.2   Twenty Years of Inflation in Selected OECD Countries   8

Chapter 2

2.1   Annual Inflation Rates, 1947-1979   17
2.2   First Differences in Log of Monthly CPI, 1967-1979   19
2.3   Anticipated and Unanticipated Inflation in Semiannual
      Livingston Surveys   29

Chapter 3

3.1   Bias Factor for Omission as a Function
      of Omitted-Included Correlation   56
3.2   Bias Factor for Omission as a Function
      of Standard Deviations   57
3.3   Monthly Effect of Omitting Apparel   62
3.4   Quarterly Effect of Omitting Apparel   63
3.5   Annual Effect of Omitting Apparel   64
3.6   Quarterly Effect of Omitting Cities of 50,000 to 200,000   68
3.7   Annual Effect of Omitting Cities of 1 Million to 3 Million   69
3.8   Correlation Structure Between Cities   72
3.9   Median Cross-goods Autocorrelation   74
3.10 Monthly Quality Adjustment for Refrigerators   82
3.11 One-lag Autocorrelation Plot for WPI Component   83
3.12 Annual Effects for Specific Errors, Absolute Scale   90
3.13 Annual Effects for Specific Errors, Logarithmic Scale   91
3.14 Quarterly Effects for Specific Errors   92
3.15 Monthly Effects for Specific Errors   93
3.16 Combined Effects   95

vii

Chapter 4

4.1   Channels for International Influences   118
4.2   Temporary Price Level and Real Income Effects from an
      Unexpected Adverse Change in the Terms of Trade   124
4.3   Once-and-for-all Shift in m^d at Time t 126

Chapter 5

5.1   The Marginal Federal Income Tax Rate of the
      United States   137
5.2   Distortion of the Saving Decision   139
5.3   Four Scenarios for the Marginal Tax Rate
      on Income from Capital   144
5.4   Four Possible Trajectories for the Growth Rate of
      Detrended Output per Worker   146
5A.1 The Optimal Path of Accumulation   154
5A.2 The Optimal Accumulation Path When
      the Marginal Tax Rate is Rising   157

Chapter 6

6.1   Parallel Growth Does Not Imply Causality   173
6.2   A Common Periodic Structure Does Not Imply
      Causality   174
6.3   Schema of Effects on Inflation   176
6.4   Growth of M1 vs. CPI Inflation, 1959-1979   184

List of Tables

Chapter 1

1.1	Correlations Between Inflation Rates, 1948-1979	4
1.2	Differences Between Inflation Rates, 1948-1979	5

Chapter 3

3.1	Example Relationships Between Nominal Price and CPI	58
3.2	Amounts of Omitted Goods	61
3.3	Major Commodity Correlations	66
3.4	Omitted Consumers, by Time	67
3.5	Size Class Correlations	70
3.6	Quarterly Time Period Mismatch, Three-month Staggering	71
3.7	Correlations for Laspeyeres and COL Indexes	75
3.8	Correlations for Dynamic Concepts	77
3.9	Quality Adjustment Studies	80
3.10	Magnitude of Sampling Errors	85
3.11	Correlations Used for Extrapolation	88
3.12	Effects of Uncorrected Errors	96
3.13	Effects for Specific Price Series	96

Chapter 4

4.1	Beta Coefficients for the Nominal Supply Reaction Function	121
4.2	Summary Statistics for Prediction of Inflation Rates $\Gamma_j P$ as $\Gamma_j M - \mu$	128
4.3	Summary Statistics for Prediction of Inflation Rates by $\Gamma_j P = \sum_{i=0}^{4/j} k_i \Gamma_j M_{-ij} - \mu$	129

x   *List of Tables*

Chapter 5

5.1   Initial Percentage Increases in Consumption   147
5.2   Percentage Reduction in the Steady-State Capital Stock   149
5.3   Percentage Reduction in the Steady-State
       Level of Consumption   150
5.4   Compensation for Inflation as a Percent
       of Consumption in 1972   152
5B.1   Net Income from Capital in 1972   159

Chapter 6

6.1   Causality Results Between Various Economic Indicators
       and the Monetary Aggregates   180
6.2   Simulation of Price-Ml Equation, 1971-III to 1975-IV   186
6.3   Simulations of Price-Ml Equation over 1978-1980 Period
       and Comparison to Forecasts by Major Analysts   188

Preface

The papers in this volume were prepared following a symposium at the annual meeting of the American Association for the Advancement of Science in January 1980. My intention in arranging that symposium was to present some reviews and highlights of recent work on inflation. I selected participants from industry, academia, and government so that a variety of viewpoints would be presented.

I had hoped that the papers would make recent economic research results more available to the noneconomist. However, they will have more interest to the professional macroeconomist. All the papers contain new results, and those by Carlson and Gale contain in-depth reviews of specific areas. Economics students may find the collection useful because of the particularly careful expositions of background and methodology. The noneconomist should have no trouble understanding the introduction, as well as some sections in each paper.

I thank Gardner Ackley, George Bach, Robert Hall, Randall Hinshaw, Michael Keran, and John Shoven for their suggestions while I was arranging the symposium. I again thank the authors and Paul Earl for their participation in the symposium, and Michael Darby for his counsel while I was preparing the book.

The book was typeset in Times Roman Font by Bell Laboratories TROFF computer program. Thanks are due Carmella Patuto and Patty McCrea for their fine jobs of typing and correcting the manuscript.

William A. Gale

1

Introduction

William A. Gale

Since the early 1970's, the American public has regarded inflation as the outstanding economic problem. Candidates for office, sensitive to the concern, berate the ineffectual actions of the incumbents and promise to eliminate it. Incumbents try one action after another. Yet in that decade, inflation has only become worse. Why? Has there been a lack of understanding of the causes or consequents of inflation? a lack of will or power to control it? The mismatch between concern and lack of results surely deserves investigation.

The papers in this book address several key issues raised by persisting inflation in the economy. They cannot and do not, in this space, present a complete argument, but they do bring quantitative evidence to bear on important issues. They form part of an argument that inflation can and should be controlled.

Economists assume that the public perceives the problem as one of a rising general price level. They distinguish this from a change in relative prices, and point out that while relative prices can change even in a barter economy, a rise in all prices requires a monetary economy. John Carlson's paper, the second chapter in this volume, reviews what economists know about how the public and economists perceive inflation, and how they both form expectations of inflation.

Carlson shows that perceptions of what has happened vary a great deal from person to person. For the general public, perceptions vary because of using different goods, shopping in different stores, and buying at different times; also, some people are older and have a longer period to base their judgments on. Still, recent price changes do seem to be reflected in the public's perceptions and expectations.

Economists also differ in how they perceive and predict inflation, but less so than the public. They are more aware of aggregate measures, such as the Consumer Price Index, so their perceptions of the past are much more similar than the public's are. But they still form different models and arrive at different expectations. One study showed that economists' expectations were persistently too low, that simple models would have had less error. But Carlson points out that the "simple model" against which we could compare the economists predictions is formed after all the data are in. It is never so clear at the moment what is a good model. A model published in 1972, for instance, gave a good fit by supposing that inflation rates tended back to some level. This model no longer fits so well, and the recent models have a different form.

The system that economists are attempting to understand is constantly changing. In particular, it is changed by what they find. Economists can rarely find room for planned experiments, and frequently they cannot even measure what they are interested in except over rather long periods, such as a year. As a result, they need to study a period of decades in order to obtain reliable statistical evidence of what has happened. What is available, then, is some perception of the average process during the period of the study, which is, of course, no longer the current process. For this reason, there is considerable room for informed and honest people to differ over what the current system is and what should be done. Carlson's paper is very useful for showing how economists form these differing perceptions.

Economists' perceptions of inflation rest on measurements of the "general price level" and on rates of change of price indexes. The thousands of goods and services in a modern economy make any price level measurement a formidable organizational and technical problem. However, price level measurement is accomplished not just by one organization, but by several, which necessitates a choice among the alternatives. Three widely used indexes of the general price level in the United States are the Consumer Price Index (CPI), the Implicit Deflator for the Gross National Product (GNPD), and the Producer Price Index for Finished Goods (PPFG).

These three price indexes are defined differently, published by different groups of people, and designed for different purposes, but their results are not actually very different. The CPI, published monthly by a group within the Bureau of Labor Statistics (BLS), was founded to give some guidance to setting wages for shipbuilders during the World War I period of inflation. Since then, it has been expanded and refined many times, but one of its major uses continues to be wage adjustment. Conceptually, the CPI is an average of the prices of all goods purchased by consumers, each item weighted by the total amount spent for it. In practice, some goods are chosen to represent a multitude of goods, and the CPI is an average of the prices of the representative goods, each good weighted by the total amount spent on the goods it represents. The total amounts spent have been determined by irregularly scheduled massive surveys of consumer purchases. The weights and representative goods change a few years after each survey. For example, the most recent change was effective January 1978, based on a survey done in 1972-1973. On the other hand, prices are gathered monthly from about 20,000 stores in eighty-five urban areas throughout the country. The CPI is a reasonable choice of a price index when the focus of a study is on the consumer, as in an analysis of demand or a comparison of wages across time.

The GNPD is calculated quarterly within the Bureau of Economic Analysis (BEA). Its primary purpose is to allow comparison of the GNP across time. The GNPD expresses the ratio between the values of a given flow of all final goods and services as calculated using (1) current prices and (2) historical prices. The GNPD is broader than the CPI in its coverage of final goods and services, most importantly because it covers government provided goods and services. It also differs from the CPI in that it attempts to estimate only the prices of currently produced goods and services. Accordingly, the treatment of durable goods such as housing and automobiles is conceptually different. Another difference is that the GNPD uses weights as observed each quarter, so a special survey is not needed. In practice, it is based largely on data gathered by the BEA for the CPI and the Producer Price Indexes (PPI). About 95 percent of the weight in the Personal Consumption Expenditures category of the GNP uses the same price information gathered for the CPI, while the deflator for the government sector is calculated using PPI component series. The calculation procedures are different, of course. The GNPD is a reasonable choice for a study that focuses on both personal and government expenditures.

The Producer Price Indexes are published by another group within the BLS. They are primarily intended to be used at a low level of aggregation, for example, to adjust a contract for buying steel or to compare a particular firm's input prices across time. However, some aggregates of the PPI are published. Of these, the index for finished goods (the PPFG) most nearly matches the notion of an index of output prices. The price data for the PPI come from producers rather than from retailers. The weighting of the prices is derived from the value of shipments made during an economic census; the weights thus remain fixed, as they do in the CPI, but because producers supply the price information, the weights are not based on the consumption of goods. A problem with the prices gathered for the PPI (and used in the GNPD) is that there is an almost equal mixture of "order" prices — in effect when the goods were ordered — and "shipment" prices — in effect on the shipping date. Twelve percent of time lags between order and shipment are greater than six months and 60 percent are more than one month but less than six. The PPFG might be considered in a study that focuses on a business.

Despite the differences in these indexes, the annual inflation rates measured by each over the last three decades have been quite similar. Table 1.1 shows correlations for the annual inflation rates from the three price measures.

Table 1.1

Correlations Between Inflation Rates, 1948-1979

	CPI	GNPD	PPFG
CPI	1.00	.96	.94
GNPD		1.00	.95
PPFG			1.00

The high correlations show that the measures agree on which years inflation is high and which years it is low. The differences between the correlations are not significant. The measures also agreed on the average inflation rate from 1948 to 1979. Table 1.2 shows some summary statistics formed by subtracting the CPI from each of the other series. The two means shown do not differ significantly from zero. Thus, the choice between these measures of inflation is more a matter of aesthetics in conforming to a theory than of practical difference.

Table 1.2

Differences between Inflation Rates, 1948-1979

	Mean %/yr	S. D. of Mean %/yr	S. D. of Differences %/yr
I(GNPD) - I(CPI)	.11	.17	.94
I(PPFG) - I(CPI)	−.35	.26	1.45

Chapter 3 in this volume is a detailed examination of the errors in using the CPI as a measure of inflation. For the economist, the greatest cost of inflation may be error introduced in any time series study by errors in measuring inflation! The cost is the inability to see economic processes over time clearly and without bias. The paper is the first attempt to systematically quantify the errors in measuring inflation. It finds that for monthly measures of inflation, the error exceeds the signal. That is, we do not have individual monthly measures of inflation. For quarterly use the signal is about 1.5 times the noise — suitable for use only with great caution. *Noise* and *signal* are variances, defined in detail in the chapter. For annual use, however, the signal is over ten times the noise. This structure of signal-to-noise ratio results not from different or better procedures for annual data, but from the smaller importance of the same errors, which in turn occurs because even unrelated price changes show increasing correlations as the time period increases. Apparently there *is* something general about a general price increase, at least over periods as great as a year.

In Carlson's paper, the figures give a nice overview of inflation in the United States in the last few decades. Two other figures may be useful in understanding the public concern with inflation. Figure 1.1 shows a hundred-year overview of inflation in the United States. The data, pieced together by Klein (1975), represent the deflator for net national product. The errors in the early terms of this series can only be guessed, of course. The annual inflation rates are plotted by asterisks, with a smoothed curve drawn through them. If we accept the data, what they show is that the recent inflation has been the highest peacetime inflation in the hundred years. The inflation accompanying

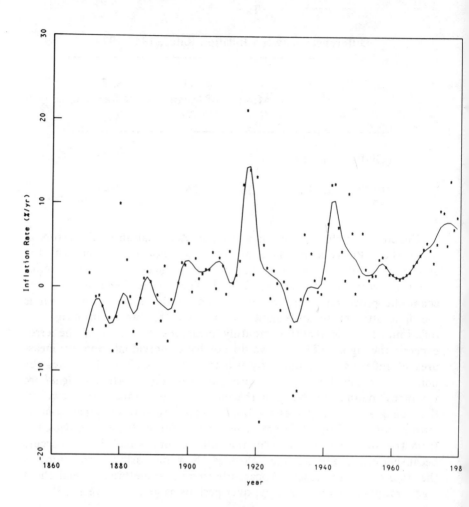

Figure 1.1
Hundred-year Overview of U.S. Inflation

the two world wars stands out also, and there is an apparent change from a rather cyclic pattern before World War I to a less cyclic behavior after World War II.

Figure 1.2 compares inflation rates in eight other Organization for Economic Cooperation and Development (OECD) countries and the United States during the last two decades. The inflation rates for each country were calculated from the consumer price indexes published by the OECD Director of Information (1980). The countries were selected for geographical dispersion. The inflation rates for each year are plotted radially, counterclockwise, starting with 1961 horizontally to the right. The scales are the same for each star figure. Most of the countries show a pattern of considerably greater inflation in the last five to ten years than in the early sixties. A way of expressing the similarity to the U.S. pattern is this: the average inflation rates for the other eight countries shown explains 65 percent of the variance in the U.S. inflation rate. This is an observation without a theory, but it may lie behind a common feeling that U.S. inflation has been imported and is therefore not under control. The figure also shows 1974, the year of the first oil crunch, to have been a particularly bad year for several countries, leading to discussion of oil price increases as a cause of inflation.

In Chapter 4, Michael Darby examines closely the possible causation of U.S. inflation by international events. He rejects the notion of international causation, finding that external events add little to the explanation that internal factors cause U.S. inflation.

Darby distinguishes the short term effect for impulses such as the 1974 oil price rise from its long term effect. In the short term, a weighted index of prices, such as the CPI, will rise when one of the components increases. But in the long run, unless there is an accommodative rise in the money supply, some other prices must fall to clear all markets. The result should be no rise in the average of prices. The empirical results that Darby presents show that four-year inflation rates can be explained solely by the four-year growth of the U.S. money supply, and that the international events add nothing to the explanation. He concludes that we can look only to ourselves for responsibility for the past inflation, but that accordingly we should be able to determine our inflation rate in the future.

Public concern with inflation assumes that inflation has bad consequences. It is perhaps remarkable, therefore, that economists have a wide range of opinions on this proposition. There is, in fact,

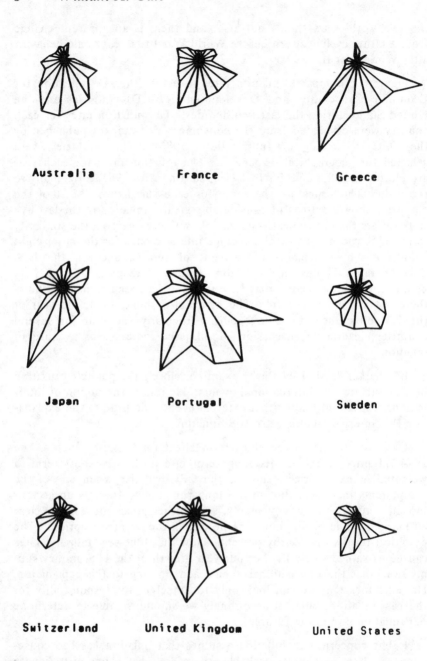

Figure 1.2
Twenty Years of Inflation in Selected OECD Countries

widespread agreement that if transaction costs were zero, a completely anticipated inflation, affecting all goods and services equally, would not affect individual or aggregate welfare. However, only recently have the obvious deviations from these three conditions been systematically set out (Fischer and Modigliani, 1978), with much research still to be done and many effects still to be quantified. Perhaps the most attention has been given to effects rising from the U.S. government's failure to index its tax laws, or to accommodate the actual inflation fully (Nowotny, 1980). Paul Evans, in Chapter 5, observes that marginal tax rates for individuals have risen due to inflation. He argues that a higher marginal tax rate leads to greater current consumption, less savings, and lowered later consumption. The net effect he shows must be negative. He also attempts a quantification of the effects to be expected from a rising marginal tax rate. The model he uses to do this is the simplest that can capture the effect he discusses, and it therefore lacks many elements of realism. It is, however, parameterized to simulate the U.S. economy. Evans finds that people would be indifferent to a great depression or to a repeated unaccommodated inflation like that of the 1970s. The sensitivity of this rough description of his results to the less certain parameters in his model is low. This is, needless to say, a controversial result. However, since it represents a modern supply-side argument, it needs to be considered and the assumptions necessary for the result need to be elicited. For contrast with an older viewpoint, consider Robert Solow's (1975) judgment of the same effect:

> So taxpayers suffer a loss in purchasing power after taxes, and their loss is the Treasury's gain. Not good, one is tempted to say, but no worse than a bad cold. Real GNP, for all its faults, is the best measure we have of the current production of valued goods and services; that's the number to watch.

The difference between Evans's "bad as a great recession" and Solow's "no worse than a bad cold" is that Solow does not seem to think that a higher inflation rate will retard the growth rate, while Evans gives a reason for thinking that it will.

As with any perceived problem, concern with inflation is translated into attempts to prevent it or to cushion its consequences. The first empirical question is whether inflation can be controlled. The nature of the evidence should be that something controllable affects the amount of inflation, and is at the same time not forced to react to other problems. In the final chapter, Michael Bazdarich assumes that the "something controllable" is the money supply. He investigates empirically the extent to which money supply reacts to a variety of other economic variables.

The crucial empirical task here is to demonstrate whether or not something "affects" the money supply. What is needed is a causality test. This kind of test has occupied much of economic thinking with many disputes turning on a causality interpretation. Bazdarich has applied a recent form of causality tests to a variety of inflation measures, money supply measures, and cost measures. The tests are designed to eliminate positive readings merely because two variables increase together, and to give a positive reading only if there is an influence of one variable on another after accounting for the other's own past history.

The results of his tests as set out in his Table 6.1 are reasonably clear. Money supply has not been accommodating the other variables he examined, which included unemployment, government deficit, government spending, wage rates, and a variety of price measures. On the other hand, the same table shows that money supply growth rate changes have affected the various price measures. This is a key link in some arguments that inflation can be controlled.

In summary, the argument suggested by these papers, though not fully developed, is as follows. Inflation expectations are diffuse and hard to measure, but they do rise when inflation has increased. Public concern with inflation is assumed to be a concern with a rising general price level. We can measure price-level changes on an annual basis, and therefore we can study its causes and consequents. The causes of our inflation have been domestic, not international. A consequence of higher inflation has been a rising marginal tax rate which has been responsible for declining economic growth. The money supply growth rate affects the inflation rate and does not have to respond to other economic variables. The completed argument would assert that inflation can and should be controlled.

References

Fischer, S., and F. Modigliani. 1978. "Towards an Understanding of the Real Effects and Costs of Inflation." *Weltwistschafliches Archiv* 114, pp. 810-833.

Klein, B. 1975. "Our New Monetary Standard: The Measurement and Effects of Price Uncertainty." *Economic Inquiry* 13, pp. 461-484.

Nowotny, E. 1980. "Inflation and Taxation — Reviewing the Macroeconomic Issues." *Journal of Economic Literature* 18, pp. 1025-1049.

OECD Director of Information. 1980. *Consumer Price Indices: sources and methods and historical statistics*, Special Issue, Paris.

Solow, Robert. 1975. "The intelligent citizen's guide to inflation", *The Public Interest*, 38 (Winter), pp. 30-66.

2

Perceptions (or Misperceptions) of Inflation

John A. Carlson

Purdue University

1. Introduction

Inflation expectations can be self-fulfilling prophecies. This claim appears to be widely believed. The general idea is that if prices are expected to rise at a rate of, say, 10 percent per year, most businesses will plan to raise their own prices at about that rate and grant similar wage increases to employees. Monetary policymakers are then confronted with a dilemma: either expand the money supply sufficiently so that demand will be high enough to absorb the goods produced at the higher prices, or keep down the growth in the money supply, which will cause shortfall in demand and a subsequent collapse in output and employment. If policymakers choose to keep up demand, the inflation expectations may turn out to be approximately correct.

One of the more compelling arguments in favor of wage-price controls rests on this idea. If most people can be convinced that the rise in prices will be limited by controls, they will be less reluctant to accept smaller wage increases. Then costs do not rise quickly and price increases can be restrained in accordance with controls without unduly

13

squeezing profits or forcing bankruptcies.

The foregoing line of reasoning involves a number of controversial issues. Here we shall concentrate primarily on reviewing some of the literature that pertains to the key issue of whether there is such a thing as an expected rate of inflation. A number of questions will motivate the discussion. What influences how quickly people expect prices to rise? Is there usually a consensus about this? If so, how does it come about? If not, why do different people have different expectations?

We shall take the position that each person has a "model" of how the world works. This may vary from extremely naive to highly sophisticated. Any model involves hypothesized relationships and data or observations on which forecasts of the future may be based. In the case of inflation, important pieces of data are the rates of inflation that have been observed or perceived to have existed in the past. An aspect of this, to be developed in more detail later, is that these perceptions may or may not be correct.

As for hypothesized relationships, consider the analogy of predicting the ocean's tide. A person may see a rising tide for the first time and expect it will continue to rise. When he sees the tide stop rising and start falling, he will probably change his prediction and say that the tide will fall, at least for a while. With observations that have timed the rise and fall of several tides, a turning point can be predicted, perhaps not precisely, but with some confidence that it will occur within a specifiable interval. With only a few observations, however, projections well into the future may not be very good if changing weather conditions have interfered with the determination of when the tides actually changed. A more sophisticated model based on the gravitational pull of the moon and knowledge of the moon's rotational pattern around the earth allow for even better predictions of the changing tides far into the future.

The point of this analogy is not to suggest that economists have come close to a theory that can forecast inflation with much accuracy. Rather, it is to highlight how forecasts depend on hypothesized relationships, as well as observations, that may differ markedly from individual to individual. Inflation is a complicated phenomenon, so it is not surprising that there are different perceptions of what is involved.

We begin our review in Section 2 with a historical look at the recent U.S. experience with inflation. As we look at the evidence that inflation does not proceed smoothly, we can begin to get a better idea about why so much uncertainty surrounds how quickly prices have been rising and how quickly they can reasonably be expected to rise in the future. Confusion is compounded by the fact that prices of different commodities often undergo dramatically different rates of change over relatively short periods. The impact of these relative price changes on perceptions of inflation is addressed in Section 3.

Section 4 turns to survey evidence about expectations of inflation and some of the patterns that are in evidence. An alternative to surveys, considered in Section 5, involves a statistical analysis and a belief that observed relationships in the past are generally projected into the future. It also provides some interesting information about the extent to which short-run changes in inflation might reasonably be believed to signal more permanent trends.

Several of these considerations are then brought together in Section 6. The statistical approach provides a way to analyze further the inflation expectations revealed by surveys of economic forecasters, and it provides a challenge to those who may unthinkingly believe that these expectations are likely to be representative of any set of people who form expectations about inflation. The survey evidence, in turn, raises serious questions about how appropriate it is to assume, as many economists have done, that expectations are approximately "rational." Section 6 contains a few brief concluding comments.

2. Recent U.S.Experience

Economists frequently talk about the *general price level*. What they have in mind is some index of prices, any number of which might be used. When we need a particular index for illustrative purposes, we shall use the Consumer Price Index (CPI). By the *rate of inflation* we shall mean the rate at which the general price level goes up or, more specifically, the rate of increase in the CPI.

Figures 2.1 and 2.2 have been prepared to give some idea of the inflation experience of the United States in recent years. The first one depicts annual rates of inflation and the other shows monthly inflation.

Let P_t denote the CPI reported for month t. The inflation rate has been calculated as the difference in the logarithms of the price indexes observed at two different times. Using log differences as an approximation for the percentage change has several computational advantages and is used extensively by economists modeling the inflation phenomena.

Figure 2.1 shows the annual inflation rates from 1947 to 1979. There has clearly been a strong upward trend since the early 1960s, but the overall pattern is not a smooth one. There have been upward surges in prices right after World War II, in 1950-1951 with the beginning of the Korean War, in the late 1960s with the increasing U.S. military involvement in Vietnam, again in 1973-1974, and most recently in the late 1970s.

These upward surges have been interrupted by the onset of, or immediately following, recessions in 1949, 1953-1954, 1957-1958, 1960, 1970, and 1974-1975. But each successive decline in the inflation rate was to a higher plateau, from which a new wave of inflation took off during the subsequent recovery phase of the business cycle. Without additional information, the inference we could draw from these patterns is that it may take a serious, sustained recession to reverse this trend and bring inflation back down to the low levels of the early 1950s.

Taking a closer look at the twelve years from 1967-1979, we can see three distinct, upward movements in the inflation rate. The first in the late 1960s, as we said, was associated with the war in Vietnam. Inflation came down slightly in 1970 but was still above 5 percent. A further decline took place in 1971-1972 along with the U.S. experiment with wage-price controls. It is difficult to assess how much of that might have occurred anyway and how much was postponed until controls began to break down in 1973 and finally came off in 1974.

The runup of prices in 1973-1974 was aggravated by crop failures around the world in 1973 and the oil embargo later that year. The sharp recession in late 1974 was followed by a moderating of inflation in 1975 and 1976. In the next three years, however, inflation has taken off again, reaching a high of 13 percent in 1979, and staying almost that high in 1980 despite a recession.

Superimposed on these annual rates of inflation is a jagged pattern of monthly changes, as seen for the 1967-1979 period of Figure 2.2. In that figure the differences in the logs of the price index on successive months has been multiplied by 12 to indicate the inflation at an annual rate (if it were to continue for twelve months at the same monthly rate).

In Figure 2.2, the three surges of inflation are perceptible but far less dramatic, being masked by the month-to-month gyrations. It now becomes very difficult with only monthly data from the past to tell whether the latest change signals the beginning of a new trend or is just

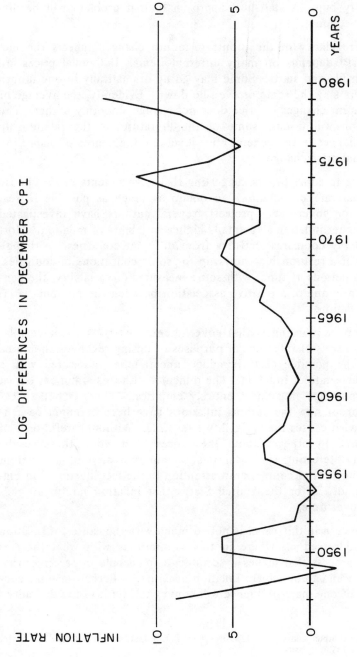

Figure 2.1
Annual Inflation Rates, 1947-1979

a temporary blip. A statistical approach to that problem will be discussed in Section 4.

This irregularity in the month-to-month changes reflects the fact that the CPI depends on many different items. Individual prices are changed in fits and starts. Some may go up dramatically in one month while others stay the same or even go down. Evidently, the average of these different changes in price does not change smoothly, either. The next section will discuss some of the literature on the relationship between changes in the general price level and the degree of dispersion in individual price changes.

Reacting to some papers suggesting that governments might choose an "optimal rate of inflation" to obtain as much as possible in real resources for government projects, several authors have investigated whether higher inflation also entails higher variability of inflation.[1] Most of this simply compares statistics from different countries. Although not much of a relationship shows up for some collections of countries, over some periods of time, with some measures of variability, the general pattern is one of a positive association between the rate and variability of inflation.

The implied warning is that governments that try to achieve relatively high levels of inflation for purposes of raising revenues should be aware of the possible costs in added uncertainties associated with a more variable rate of inflation. The difficulty with this argument is that the underpinnings are almost entirely empirical. There is not a clear specification of how the various inflations have been or might be generated or what causes the variability over time. Without careful tests of well-specified hypotheses about the processes at work, these results remain an interesting statistical relationship in search of a coherent theory. They do, of course, draw attention to the fact illustrated in Figures 2.1 and 2.2 for the United States that inflation rarely proceeds smoothly over time.

The concern in this paper is not so much with the causes of inflation (a topic addressed elsewhere in this volume) as with what there is about the process that makes it so difficult for people to perceive what is going on and to anticipate inflation accurately. Perhaps a brief consideration of one major influence will convey the spirit of the difficulty.

---

1. See, for example, Okun (1971), Gordon (1971), Logue and Willett (1976), Foster (1979), and Gale (1980).

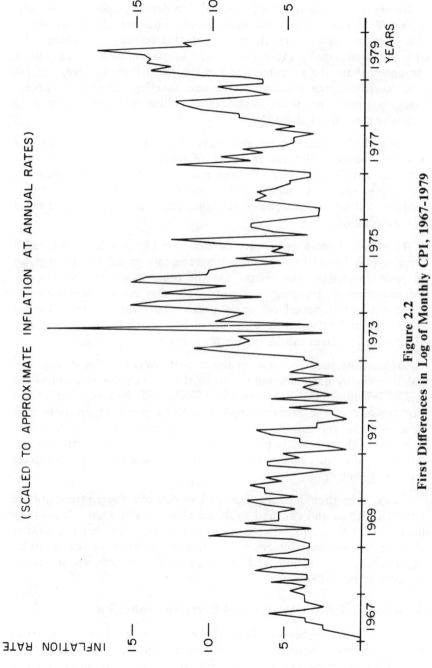

Figure 2.2

First Differences in Log of Monthly CPI, 1967-1979

Before a meeting of OPEC ministers to decide prices of crude oil, there will be considerable speculation and conjecture about how much of a price increase to expect, how much that increase will change the CPI, and how rapidly these effects will be transmitted. Even with a consensus about the probable size and timing of these changes, uncertainty surrounds the outcome of the next meeting; despite this uncertainty, contracts for future payments are often made on the basis of traders' expectations about the future.

Once the ministers meet and make their announcement, there is new information. Suppose the price increase is more than had been generally anticipated. The expected prices of future commodities will probably be revised upward, and contracts for future delivery of various products will now be negotiated at higher prices as a reflection of these new expectations.

There still remain great uncertainties. On the one hand, future oil supplies may be cut because of tacit agreements or political turmoil, so oil prices may rise even faster. On the other hand, new supplies or reduced demand, bringing on a glut of oil, may cause a breakdown of the cartel and an actual fall in oil prices. Therefore, it will take still more time and information to ascertain how much of the current rate of oil price increases can be reasonably expected to continue.

Similar uncertainties hold for the rate of growth of the money supply, thought by many economists to be the primary determinant of the rate of inflation. The link between inflation and the rate of growth in any measure of the money supply cannot be predicted precisely over short intervals and can change over longer periods. There is the added uncertainty about possible policy changes if new events convince monetary authorities to change existing policies or when new policymakers are put in control.

Thus, even though over longer periods one can discern trends in the rate of inflation and can find evidence of some statistical relationships between inflation and other data, knowing what will happen next is clouded by unknown future events, lack of precision in the statistical explanations for inflation, and short-run confusion even about what is the current rate of inflation.

3. Relative Price Changes and Perceived Inflation

Part of the confusion about the current rate of inflation arises because different people receive different information about what is happening to prices and may often interpret that information in vastly

Sampling theory suggests there will be different perceptions even about the current prices of particular commodities. For example, when unemployed workers search for a type of job by checking the wages at a sample of firms, then the average wage and the highest wage found by different individuals will have distributions that depend on the distribution of actual wages and the nature of the sampling process. Similar considerations apply to perceptions of buyers who sample prices but do not canvass an entire set of sellers before making a purchase.

When it comes to assessing what is happening to the average price of a whole bundle of different commodities, the fact of diverse information becomes even more dramatic. Whether a household is assessing its own budget or managers in firms are trying to determine the costs of raw materials or the prices that their competitors are setting, it is certainly true that different economic agents will have widely diverse bits of information about components of any general index of prices.

There is no doubt that relative prices change unevenly over time. Technological breakthroughs and enlarged scales of production often enable items that were once very expensive to be produced more cheaply. Witness the decline in prices of small electronic calculators a few years ago. Video recorders may exhibit the same phenomenon even when most other prices are going up rapidly. Shortages develop for some items and their prices may soar, as occurred with agricultural products in 1973. These are just a few examples of relative price changes.

A *relative price* refers to the ratio of the price of one commodity to that of another. They are always changing, but do they change more in inflationary than in noninflationary times? Lucas (1976), for example, has stated that he sees no reason for the variation in relative prices to be systematically related to variations in the general price level. Since data are available on prices of different kinds of commodities, this sort of claim can be examined empirically.

Vining and Elwertowski (1976) show, using the prices of components of both the Wholesale Price Index and the Consumer Price Index, that there are greater relative price changes during periods in which the price indexes also undergo the largest changes.

This is not a recent phenomenon, nor is it confined to the United States. Much earlier, Mills (1927) found a strong statistical association between the dispersion of price changes and the size of the absolute change in the price level, whether up or down. Glejser (1965) found a significant association across countries between inflation rates and relative price changes. Parks (1978) showed a similar relationship with data from the Netherlands from 1921 to 1963.

Parks's main concern, however, now that people have come to anticipate continuing inflation, is to see whether it is inflation per se or unanticipated inflation that is primarily associated with relative price instability. A good theoretical case can be made that relative price changes should not be much affected by fully anticipated changes in the average of all prices.

Later sections will consider issues about how to measure anticipated inflation. Parks uses a statistical times-series approach (see Section 5) to infer an expected rate of inflation at different times. The difference between the actual inflation and his estimate of expected inflation yields a series of observations of unanticipated inflation. In his regressions, Parks finds a strong statistical association between the variation in relative prices and the square of unanticipated inflation, a result similar to Mills's and to the claims by Vining and Elwertowski. Parks also finds that relative prices may be associated with anticipated inflation, although the relationship is much weaker. These interpretations, of course, require accepting that his time-series forecasts do reflect a widely held consensus about anticipated inflation.

Vining and Elwertowski question which way causation runs. Do changes in aggregate demand generate the divergent price responses in different sectors, or do shocks to relative prices lead to price level changes? They seem to opt for the latter view, "that an autonomous increase in relative price change dispersion somehow induces instability in the change in the general price level," (1976, p, 707) but they consider it a major challenge for future work to discriminate between these possibilities.

Cukierman (1979) objects to this way of posing the problem. An economist who wishes to account for price changes should develop a model in which individual prices are determined. Then, as the exogenous variables (influences not explained by the model) change, the model should predict what happens to individual prices. Dispersion of relative price changes and a price index are simply functions of the individual prices. Thus, the relationship between relative price dispersion and price-level changes can be inferred by analyzing the effects of variations in these outside influences.

Cukierman and Wachtel (1979) have such a model, a refinement of an earlier one by Lucas (1973). They distinguish between aggregate demand, which is an influence common to all markets, and relative demand shocks, specific to individual markets. Supply and demand in each market determine the price in that market. The variance of the aggregate demand term and the variance of the specific demand shocks are given exogenously. As the variance of aggregate demand rises, then in this model both the variation in the price level and the dispersion of relative prices increase. That relationship is the usual empirical finding. A change in the variance of relative demand shocks may or may not work in the same direction.

Cukierman's point is that causality runs from influences outside of an economic model that purports to explain prices rather than one way or the other between functions of prices that are determined by the model. He does raise one possibility in which it might be said that relative demand disturbances cause general inflation. This could occur when policymakers respond with bigger changes in aggregate demand when there are greater relative shocks to different sectors. He cites papers by Schultze (1959) and Solow (1975) that take this view.

In any event, relative prices do change, and the distribution of those changes can be markedly different at different times. Vining and Elwertowksi report that the distribution of individual price changes is generally skewed, with some indication that the direction of skew is the same as the change in the rate of inflation. The skewness is particularly pronounced during periods of rapid inflation.

This means that people will be affected differently and may have very different perceptions of the inflation process. Michael (1979) addresses the question about differential impacts on family budgets during the period from 1967 to 1974. Taking the bundle of commodities that each family purchased, as reported to the Bureau of Labor Statistics, he found a considerable dispersion in the changes in the costs of purchasing those bundles. For example, in the first six months of 1974 — a mere half-year — there was a range from a 2-percent increase to a 13-percent increase, with a standard deviation of 1.2 percent.

Michael also finds sizable and statistically significant differences in inflation's impact in any subperiod on families with different characteristics, such as income level, age, children, and so on. However, very little of this holds up consistently from one period to the next. There is much more dispersion in inflation's impact on families within groups than between groups. That raises questions about the representativeness of any group-specific index. Furthermore, differential effects one period are often reversed in another period, and families do have the option of changing the bundle of commodities they buy as relative prices change.

In view of these different experiences, it is not surprising that people have different views about inflation. This has been documented in a study in Sweden. Jonung (1981) gives some preliminary results of a massive survey of about 6000 families in early 1978. One of the questions asked was what they thought the rate of inflation had been in 1977. On average, men thought it had been 13.8 percent while women thought it had been 15.5 percent. If Swedish women do most of the food purchasing, this might be explained by the fact that in 1977 the actual rate of the inflation was 16.7 percent for food prices and 14.2 percent for all consumer prices.

While the average of these perceptions of inflation were not far off from reported figures, they mask considerable variation. The standard deviation in the men's perceived rate of inflation was 5.65 percent and for women it was 8.58 percent. For women this means that plus or minus two standard deviations would encompass perceptions that prices may not have risen at all to a belief that prices had gone up by more than 30 percent.

At first, it may seem strange that people have such wildly different perceptions of something that is as widely reported as the most recent rate of inflation. But not all people read or hear these reports, and many do not remember or perhaps even believe them. Their own experience tells them something else. They may also be highly selective in their perceptions. If the cost of a major item in the budget, such as transportation, has recently gone up 50 percent, it may seem as if everything has gone up 50 percent. As noted previously, there are often dramatically different individual price changes in relatively short periods of time, and these changes apparently carry great weight in people's perceptions of what is going on.

4. Survey Evidence of Expected Inflation

What people expect the inflation rate to be is difficult to ascertain. Economists have used two basic procedures. The first is to conduct surveys, asking a sample of individuals what they think will happen to prices during a certain period of time. The second is to assume that expectations are formed in accordance with some function of available data, and to estimate the function as if prices had been correctly anticipated. We will discuss this latter procedure in some detail in the next section, after we consider the survey approach here.

Most surveys about inflation expectations around the world have been of the qualitative variety. They ask individuals whether they think prices will go up, go down, or stay the same in the next six months or year. Or they ask managers in firms whether they expect the selling prices of their products to be higher, lower, or unchanged. By making a number of assumptions, we can often estimate an average expected rate of inflation from these survey responses.[2] While there is a large and growing literature on the use of these qualitative data, we shall concentrate here on surveys that have asked for more specific forecasts.

Juster and Comment (1978) describe the efforts by the Survey Research Center (SRC) at the University of Michigan to collect information about the expectations of households about the rate of inflation. The SRC has been asking the qualitative question in quarterly surveys since the early 1950s. In 1966, the survey began to include a supplementary question about how large a price increase was expected, specifying categories of 1 to 2 percent, 3 to 4 percent, and so on. Beginning in the mid-1970s respondents who said they expected prices to go up were then asked an open-ended question: "By about what percent do you expect prices to go up, on the average, during the next 12 months?" Analysis suggested that answers to the open-ended question better reflected people's expectations. All of those surveyed since the third quarter of 1977 have been asked the open-ended question.

These SRC responses, as well as some similar data analyzed by Defris and Williams (1979) for Australia, indicate a wide array of expectations. For example, in SRC's survey in the fourth quarter of 1977, the mean forecast of inflation for the next year was about 7 percent, but the standard deviation was over 7 percent. The distribution is highly skewed. Two percent thought prices would go down. More than 14 percent thought they would remain the same, and 2 percent didn't know whether prices would go up or down. Still another 2 percent anticipated price increases of 30 percent or more. This distribution is much more spread out than if it simply reflected the experience that families have had with their own purchases, as Michael's study indicated.

The strongest influence on the distribution of reported expectations appears to be the distribution of reported perceptions of inflation. Jonung's study in Sweden provides evidence of this. In regressions designed to account for differences in expected inflation for 1978, the

---

2. See, for example, DeMenil and Bhalla (1975) for the United States, Carlson and Parkin (1975) for the United Kingdom, and Danes (1975) for Australia.

perception of inflation in 1977 was by far the dominant explanation. Those who thought inflation had been high tended to expect it to continue to be high. And the coefficient of variation (the standard deviation divided by the mean) was about the same for expectations of inflation in 1978 as it was for perceptions of inflation in 1977, for both men and women.

The apparent link between forecasts and perceptions of inflation may be, at least in part, a manifestation of what Tversky and Kahneman (1974) call "anchoring," a tendency for estimates of something to be influenced by or biased toward an initial value. Imagine two groups of people who start with about the same knowledge about the economy. If the first group is told that inflation was about 18 percent last year and the second group that it was about 12 percent, the results of psychologists' experiments would lead us to predict that the first group will make the higher forecast of inflation for next year.

Another interesting result in Jonung's regressions is that older people expect the inflation rate to be lower than younger people do, probably because they have had more experience with lower inflation rates. This indicates that experience over a lifetime, and not just the most recent statistics, can have an effect on reported expectations of inflation.

There is a serious problem involved in interpreting the responses by a wide range of people to these open-ended survey questions. Does everyone understand percentage changes? If prices seem to have gone up "a lot," someone might readily say they have gone up 50 percent or 100 percent, with little idea of what that means, and state a similar expectation for the next year. Therefore, whose expectations should we believe when we compute any average of people's inflation expectations? As economists gain experience in analyzing these data, they may learn to assess whether the outlying expectations (or any set of responses) are of importance in predicting behavior. Juster and Comment (1978) consider savings behavior a promising area to investigate. While these data may prove to be valuable in research, care should be taken in assigning quantitative weights to each response and calling one statistic (the mean) "the expected rate of inflation" and another (the variance) "the measure of uncertainty." Experimentation will obviously be necessary, but the rationale for each experiment needs to be thought through carefully.

Another survey has attracted considerable attention because it has been conducted fairly consistently and regularly for over thirty years.

Joseph Livingston, a financial columnist in Philadelphia, twice a year asks about forty to sixty-five economic forecasters what they predict will happen to a number of economic variables in the next six and twelve months. The CPI is one of the variables that has appeared in all Livingston surveys since the late 1940s.

Livingston asks the participants to give a point estimate of the CPI. Thus, it is possible, on the basis of the latest CPI figures that were available when the questionnaires were returned, to infer the expected rate of inflation of any individual response or of the consensus (mean) forecast.[3]

What sort of properties do these forecasts exhibit? For one thing, there is not nearly as much variance in the forecasts of inflation as is found in the surveys of households. This is presumably because, being knowledgeable observers of the economy, these respondents know pretty well what the rate of inflation has been in the last year or so. Since differences in perceptions of inflation account for much of the differences in a household's stated expectations, this major source of variation is not present in the Livingston surveys.

The distribution of the Livingston forecasts is also not as highly skewed as those of households. They are somewhat too skewed for it to be very likely for all of them to have come from a normal distribution; compared with evidence of households' expectations, however, normality is a relatively good assumption for the Livingston responses.[4]

This closer approximation to normality might be explained by sampling theory. We know that relative price changes can be highly skewed, particularly when there are large changes in the rate of inflation. In forming a judgment about the underlying rate of inflation, people sample from their own experience. If there is a finite variance to the distribution of what is being sampled, then by the Central Limit Theorem the sample means approach a normal distribution as the sample size increases.[5] Since the Livingston forecasters surely take more information into account than do respondents from the typical household, it is not surprising that their forecasts are closer to normally distributed.

The consensus forecasts in the Livingston surveys appear to have underestimated inflation on average, sometimes fairly substantially.

---

3. This has been reported by Carlson (1977). See also Wachtel (1977).
4. See Carlson (1975).
5. See, for example, Hogg and Craig (1970).

This can be seen, for example, in Figure 2.3, which shows the antici-pated and actual inflation in the CPI over the six-month intervals between surveys and the corresponding unanticipated inflation. Each new burst of inflation has generally not been anticipated at all well.

There have been attempts to analyze what influences the Livingston price forecasts. One by Jacobs and Jones (1980) will be discussed in some detail in Section 5. Another set of papers has been concerned with the issue of whether the Livingston forecasts can be considered rational.

"Rational expectations" is currently a lively topic in the economics literature. It was first articulated by Muth (1961) and, after receiving limited attention for about ten years, was picked up in the 1970s by Lucas (1972), Sargent (1973), and others in connection with questions about whether demand management policies have much if any effect on output and employment in an economy. The key idea is that an economic model builder should not possess any more information about how markets or economies work than the actual participants in those markets or economies. So if decisions are assumed to be based on expectations and the model predicts that these decisions will lead to possible outcomes, then the expectations should be based on knowledge of those possible outcomes, too. This has great appeal because it provides a logical principle for inferring expectations within the context of any economic model.

A closely related idea has been developed in the finance literature. Calling it "the efficient market hypothesis," Fama (1970) provides an early survey of this literature. The hypothesis, supported by studies of financial markets, is that markets (or traders) fully use any relevant information abut the course of future market prices. Any errors in market forecasts should then be attributable to events or influences that could not be foreseen at the time the forecasts were made. As a result, forecasting errors should be random variables in efficient markets.

Thus, if there is any systematic influence on something like inflation, those influences will be discovered by people whose expecta-tions matter and will be incorporated into their forecasts. One pro-cedure that has been adopted to test for rationality of inflation forecasts is to look first for evidence of systematic relationships between inflation and other available data. The rationality hypothesis is that the expecta-tions of inflation should bear essentially the same relationship to the available data as does the actual inflation. If this null hypothesis is rejected, the data are said not to satisfy rationality.

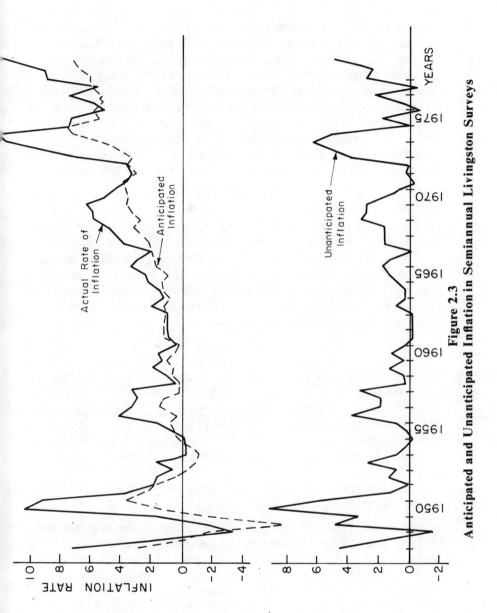

Figure 2.3

Anticipated and Unanticipated Inflation in Semiannual Livingston Surveys

Pesando (1975) conducted one such test with the Livingston data. Assuming current inflation was systematically related to inflation during the past two and a half years, he concluded that the Livingston forecasts were generally not rational. Mullineaux (1978), using the Carlson version of the Livingston forecasts challenged this conclusion. Noting a statistical problem with Pesando's procedure, Mullineaux could not reject rationality over the period for which he ran his revised tests. Despite the strong tendency for the Livingston forecasts to underestimate inflation, the actual inflation rate bore such an imprecise relationship to past inflation rates that the rationality issue was left unsettled.

Mullineaux (1980) has recently gone on to examine whether, in addition to the recent history of inflation, other variables that are believed to influence inflation had any significant effect on the Livingston forecasts. He finds that recent growth of the money supply does have an influence; but fiscal variables, such as government spending and the federal deficit, do not provide any discernible impact on inflation forecasts that are not already reflected in past inflation and money supply growth. The unemployment rate may have had some effect, but that was not terribly consistent.

Another result in Mullineaux's study worth stressing is that the "influence of both money growth and of the most recently observed inflation rate appears to have become systematically more important over time in affecting inflation expectations" (1980, p. 160). An implication is that as inflation becomes more pervasive in the U.S. economy, the forecasters pay increasing attention to recent experience and to the money supply, as evidence of its effect on inflation continues to accumulate. The message here is not to expect an invariant rule about how expectations are formed, a point emphasized by Sims (1974) and Lucas (1976). The forecasters' information-gathering process includes learning new things about a changing economy.

The main theme emerging from this review of the evidence about inflation expectations, as revealed by surveys, is that expectations do vary because of different individuals' varying experiences and perceptions. Solow (1980, p. 257) comments that "the hypothesis of rational expectations has not been able to account, so far as I know, for the wide dispersion of actually reported expectations,...except by the undocumented assumption that information sets differ. But the differences in information would have to be incredibly large to account for the observed dispersion of expectations." Without defending rational expectations, we are suggesting that perceptions of inflation based on very selective information sets may give rise to the observed variance and skewness in reported expectations. The sometimes dramatic differences in expectations can be seen not only across groups of respondents but also over time among similar respondents as conditions change.

In summary, inflation forecasts vary for at least two reasons:

(1) People are thinking about different things. Michael's study indicates how much variation there can be in the inflation rates across bundles of commodities purchased by different households. And the evidence that stated perceptions and expectations of inflation vary by even more suggests that people may focus on the prices of a still smaller set of commodities as representing "prices in general."

(2) People have different models of the inflation process on which to base projections of future inflation. Most of the survey evidence indicates that people generally forecast inflation to continue pretty much at the rate they perceive it to have been proceeding at the time, but they modify the forecast in accordance with their model and other bits of information they believe to be relevant. Jonung's study, for example, showed younger people in Sweden to have higher inflation expectations, presumably because their observations have not encompassed a "low tide" of inflation. And, according to Mullineaux's analysis, the Livingston forecasters have become increasingly sensitive to data on money supply growth.

5. Statistical Approaches to Inflation Expectations

An alternative technique for inferring the state of expectations about inflation, instead of using surveys, amounts to assuming that the expectations can be estimated from available data. This encompasses a wide variety of specific approaches, but there is a similarity to most of them.

First a researcher proposes a model of what determines inflation or what inflation is related to. (Some explicit examples will be considered shortly.) In a sense, any model put forward involves the idea of pattern recognition, of trying to discover what can be seen in retrospect to have been most useful in predicting the subsequent rates of inflation. This is what most economic forecasters do. Assuming that essentially the same relationships observed in the past will continue to hold, they project these patterns into the future. For example, a belief that the level of a price index depends primarily on the supply of money could lead a forecaster to look at how quickly the price index rises in relation to past growth rates in the money supply and to use that perceived relationship together with the latest money supply statistics to forecast how rapidly the price index will rise.

Different researchers look at different relationships. No one model has emerged as the "right" one, i.e., the one that best explains all the available data about inflation. Nevertheless, these various attempts often do lead to a better understanding of what causes inflation. When patterns appear to persist, their persistence can stimulate new hypotheses to explain them. And to the extent to which there are competing explanations, formal tests can be conducted to see which hypothesis or model better accounts for the available evidence.

In this section we will discuss in some detail examples of what are called time-series forecasts because they have been put forward as serious alternatives to survey data as a source of estimates of inflation expectations. Section 6 will consider some of the issues involved in choosing between survey data and time-series forecasts.

Time-series analysis of inflation, which precedes the time-series forecasts, usually assumes that all we need to know about inflation can be inferred from its own history without regard to other information. The main statistical problem is to detect the patterns in the history of an inflation series and to conduct some tests to be sure that the evidence is not seriously contrary to the basic hypothesis. Next, in generating forecasts, it is assumed that these patterns are generally expected to persist into the future.

To illustrate these ideas more formally, we begin with a model proposed by Muth (1960) that serves as background for other models to be presented and is of use in analyzing the problem, mentioned in Section 2, of sorting out how much of an observed change in the inflation rate from one month to the next might be considered a signal of higher future inflation on average and how much is just a temporary phenomenon. Muth incorporated the distinction between permanent and transitory shocks in the following sort of model:

$$y_t = \bar{y}_t + v_t \tag{2.1}$$

$$\bar{y}_t = \bar{y}_{t-1} + w_t \tag{2.2}$$

The variable y_t is observable. It might denote the data plotted in Figure 2.2, i.e., $y_t = \log P_t - \log P_{t-1}$. In that case, y_t is the rate of inflation in the CPI from month $t - 1$ to month t. The terms v_t and

w_t represent unobservable random variables, and $\bar{y}_t$ represents the underlying rate of inflation, which may be inferred but is not directly observed. The random variable v_t is a transitory deviation of the observed inflation from its underlying rate. Its size affects the current observation of y_t, but it has no effect on future values. By contrast, the random variable w_t is a permanent shock. If w_t is some positive (negative) number, not only the current y_t but also all future values will be permanently higher (lower) as a result.

This model of the inflation process says that inflation can be viewed as the outcome of random events. There is no reference to what causes the permanent or transitory shocks, no consideration of money supply growth, new arrangements for international pricing of oil, or changes in governments. These are all viewed, insofar as they affect the inflation rate, as random events that cannot be foretold. Even after an event occurs that might affect future inflation rates, this approach says to ignore that information until it shows up in the actual inflation series.

If one believes that this sort of statistical model adequately reflects the behavior of inflation, then it can be readily used to make projections of future inflation. Muth posed the following problem. If we have observations through period $t - 1$, what is the best forecast of y_t? Best is defined as the forecast of y_t, denoted by $\hat{y}_t$, that will minimize the mean square error. In other words, let the forecasting error be denoted by

$$a_t = y_t - \hat{y}_t \tag{2.3}$$

and choose $\hat{y}_t$ such that the expected value $E_{t-1}(a_t^2)$ is as small as possible, assuming that y_t is generated by random drawings in accordance with the model of equations (2.1) and (2.2). The subscript $t - 1$ indicates that information is available through period $t - 1$. Muth proved that the best forecasting procedure is the following rule:

$$\hat{y}_t = \theta\hat{y}_{t-1} + (1 - \theta)y_{t-1} \tag{2.4}$$

where, when v_t and w_t are independent random variables,

$$\theta = 1 + (g - (4g + g^2)^{1/2})/2 \tag{2.5}$$

and g is the ratio of the variance σ_w^2 of the permanent random term w to the variance σ_v^2 of the transitory random term v.

Equation (2.4) tells us that the new forecast is a weighted average of the last forecast and the last observation. Consider the extremes. As $\theta \rightarrow 0$, the best forecast equals the latest rate of inflation; and $\theta \rightarrow 0$ as

$g \rightarrow \infty,$

i.e., when virtually all the observed variations in the inflation rate are permanent shocks and virtually none are attributable to transitory shocks. At the other extreme, when all the variation is transitory so that $g \rightarrow 0$, then $\theta \rightarrow 1$ and most of the observed deviations from the last forecast should be ignored and treated as transitory. In that case, it is best to stick to the old forecast. Thus, as g varies from 0 the ∞, θ goes from 1 to 0.

On the basis of statistical evidence considered later, Muth's model may not be a bad hypothesis about how the monthly inflation data behave. A representative estimate of θ is .73, and from equation (2.5) that occurs when $g = .1$, so we may infer that the variance of the transitory shocks in the monthly inflation data is about ten times as large as the variance of the permanent shocks, or the ratio of the standard deviations is about three to one. Gale's estimate of monthly measurement error in this volume is fairly close to this estimate of the relative variance of transitory shocks.

Another way to view equation (2.4) is to rewrite it as

$$\hat{y}_t = \hat{y}_{t-1} + (1 - \theta)(y_{t-1} - \hat{y}_{t-1})$$

and, substituting from (2.3) for the forecasting error in period $t - 1$,

$$\hat{y}_t = \hat{y}_{t-1} + (1 - \theta)a_{t-1} \qquad (2.6)$$

This is known as an *adaptive forecast*. As new information becomes available, the last forecast is adjusted, or adapts, to the most recent error in forecasting inflation. When transitory shocks dominate and θ is relatively large (close to 1), then the forecast is adjusted by only a small fraction of the most recent error.

To recapitulate what is involved here, we start with some hypothesis of how inflation is related to available data, in this case to the past history of inflation. If we accept this hypothesis, we can use the model to project what will happen to inflation in future periods on the basis of evidence to date. We have considered explicitly only the one-period forecasts, although multiperiod forecasts can be readily constructed.

If an economist claims that the forecast implied by equation (2.4) represents expected inflation, such a claim involves assuming that people form their expectations as if they believed this model, had the proper estimate of θ, and correctly observed what the rate of inflation had been in the past. We argued in Section 4 that people apparently

have different models of the inflation process and often have perceptions that past inflation rates were very different than they actually
were. This approach assumes that somehow, on average, the relevant
expectations of inflation — whether for interest-rate determination or
wage negotiations, for example — agree with statistical forecasts. We
shall return to this idea in the next section. We now go on to a broader
view of this time-series approach to forecasting.

The standard reference for time-series analysis is a book by Box and
Jenkins (1970). They suggest viewing a series of data, such as the
monthly inflation rate, as if it were generated by one member of a wide
class of stochastic processes, called ARIMA processes. The statistical
procedure is to look at the patterns in the series and then to select the
simplest process that appears capable of generating the patterns
observed. We shall discuss briefly some simple processes that could be
or have been used with price index data. For technical details, one
should consult the Box-Jenkins book or texts devoted to time-series
analysis.

As in the discussion of Muth's model, let y_t denote the rate of
inflation in month t, $\hat{y}_t$ the forecast of y_t made with information
through month $t - 1$, and $a_t = y_t - \hat{y}_t$ the forecasting error. A critical
assumption is that a_t is an independent and identically distributed draw-
ing from some probability distribution with a mean of zero and a finite
variance.

The simplest of ARIMA processes is

$$y_t = a_t \qquad (2.7)$$

If this were the case, each observation of inflation would be independent of past inflation rates and would have an expected value of zero.
This null hypothesis can be tested against a less restrictive alternative.
If the observations appear to be highly improbable when the null
hypothesis is true, then it should be rejected. A look at Figures 2.1 and
2.2 should be enough to convince anyone that (2.7) is not a plausible
hypothesis for a statistical characterization of the recent inflation in the
United States.

Any autoregressive process (the AR in ARIMA) is one in which the
variable y_t is a linear function of earlier observations ($y_{t-1}, y_{t-2}, ...$). A
first-order autoregressive process can be written

$$y_t = \phi_0 + \phi_1 y_{t-1} + a_t \qquad (2.8)$$

where ϕ_0 and ϕ_1 are constants. If $\phi_0 = 0$ and $\phi_1 = 1$, (2.8) would be interpreted as saying this month's inflation equals last month's inflation plus a random error.

If ϕ_1 were a positive fraction, then inflation would, except for random errors, tend to gravitate toward some long-run rate. This is essentially what Nelson (1972) presents in comparing the predictive performance of a relatively complex econometric model against predictions by simple time-series models. He reports that a first-order autoregressive process was an adequate representation for the quarterly changes in a price index over the period from 1947 to 1966. In simplified form, he found:

$$y_t = .25 + .5y_{t-1} + a_t$$

where y_t in this case denotes the quarterly change in the GNP deflator (a price index that encompasses more commodities than the CPI). This can be rewritten

$$y_t = .50 + .5(y_{t-1} - .50) + a_t \tag{2.9}$$

To interpret (2.9), suppose $y_t = .5$ means that inflation is about one-half of 1 percent per quarter or about 2 percent per year. When inflation exceeds .5 in one quarter — say, equal to .9 — inflation in the next quarter is expected to be just half the difference between .9 and .5 — i.e., .7 — plus an unpredictable random term whose expected value has been assumed to be zero. Thus, in the absence of random shocks, Nelson's estimated process predicts that inflation will gravitate toward a rate of about 2 percent per year. If we look at Figure 2.1 for the 1947-1966 period, this seems like a plausible hypothesis. The inflationary shock at the beginning of the Korean War in 1950 and 1951 died away, and the slight deflation following the 1953-1954 recession was also temporary. The movement is generally around a 2-percent rate of inflation.

Consider now still another process. If the forecast errors can have a delayed impact on inflation, we have what is known as a moving-average process (the MA in ARIMA). A combination first-order autoregressive and first-order moving-average process can be written

$$y_t = \phi_0 + \phi_1 y_{t-1} + a_t - \theta a_{t-1} \tag{2.10}$$

The parameter θ from the moving-average process indicates the extent of the impact of last period's error on this period's value of y.

When equation (2.10) is fitted to the monthly inflation data from 1967 through 1979, as plotted in Figure 2.2, it appears to be an acceptable representation of the series. In other words, at conventional levels of significance, we cannot reject the hypothesis that the forecasting errors were independent random variables. The estimated value of ϕ_0 was very small and insignificantly different from zero, while ϕ_1 was about .95, but not significantly different from 1.0. The moving average coefficient θ was about .66.

These foregoing results are supportive of estimates reported by Pearce (1979). He claims, letting y_t denote the monthly change in the CPI, that inflation is adequately modeled by the following equation:

$$y_t = y_{t-1} + a_t - \theta a_{t-1} \qquad (2.11)$$

Pearce estimates this first for monthly data from 1947 to 1959 and then keeps adding six month's worth of data and re-estimating until he reaches the end of 1975. He reports that all the estimates of θ fall within the range from .71 to .76.

Equation (2.11) is essentially the same as the Muth model. Its implied forecasts are precisely the same. To see this, consider taking the expected value of y_t knowing what has happened through period $t - 1$:

$$E_{t-1}(y_t) = y_{t-1} + E_{t-1}(a_t) - \theta a_{t-1}$$

Denoting $E_{t-1}(y_t)$ by $\hat{y}_t$ and assuming that the expected value of the forecasting error is zero:

$$\hat{y}_t = y_{t-1} - \theta a_{t-1}$$

But $a_{t-1} = y_{t-1} - \hat{y}_{t-1}$ is last period's forecasting error. After substituting for a_{t-1} and rearranging terms,

$$\hat{y}_t = \theta \hat{y}_{t-1} + (1 - \theta)y_{t-1}$$

This is equation (2.6), which Muth proved was the optimal forecast given by his model.

Therefore, the θ in Pearce's moving average process may be interpreted as a function of the ratio of the variances of permanent and transitory shocks in accordance with equation (2.5). As noted previously, a value of $\theta = .73$ corresponds to the case in which the variance of transitory shocks to the monthly inflation rate is about ten times as large as the variance of the permanent shocks.

6. Survey Evidence vs. Time-Series Forecasts

The last two sections have examined (1) survey evidence about expectations and perceptions of inflation and (2) time-series forecasts that researchers assume represent average opinion. In this section, we turn to some questions that evidence from each approach raises about the other. Since we do not have definitive answers, many of the questions must be left unsettled. Posing them, however, may serve a useful purpose in focusing attention on evidence from surveys that should be adequately explained or taken into account by new models of the inflation process and on the need for surveys more carefully designed for purposes other than providing a journalist with material for an interesting article.

First we turn in some detail to a time-series analysis of the Livingston consensus forecasts to see what patterns may have been picked up on average by those surveyed. This leads us into a challenge to the relevance of the Livingston forecasts posed by Pearce and based on his time-series model considered in the last section. In evaluating this challenge with what evidence is currently available, we are led, as indicated earlier, to even more unanswered questions.

Jacobs and Jones (1980) assume that a representative respondent to the Livingston surveys perceives the evolution of the CPI as a time-series model. They propose extending the Muth model in two directions. First, they note that people personally observe prices and changes in those prices, not inflation rates, and the Livingston respondents were asked to predict the price level. So with p_t denoting the log of the CPI in month t, the first equation supposes that the observed value of p_t is equal to an underlying but unobserved level $\bar{p}_t$ plus a random term u_t. Second, they introduce the possibility of drift in the inflation rate. If prices are accelerating (i.e., if the inflation rate is getting higher), forecasters might perceive a positive drift.

The model itself can be written as follows:

$$p_t = \bar{p}_t + u_t \tag{2.12}$$

$$\bar{p}_t = \bar{p}_{t-1} + \bar{y}_t + v_t \tag{2.13}$$

$$\bar{y}_t = \bar{y}_{t-1} + \bar{d}_t + w_t \tag{2.14}$$

$$\bar{d}_t = \bar{d}_{t-1} + z_t \tag{2.15}$$

In equation (2.15), $\bar{d}_t$ denotes an underlying drift in the inflation rate, which is subject to a random change z_t. In (2.14), the underlying inflation rate $\bar{y}_t$ is equal to what it was last period plus the underlying drift plus a random influence w_t. Similarly, the underlying price level $\bar{p}_t$ is assumed in (2.13) to grow at the underlying rate of inflation plus a random shift v_t. This model reduces to Muth's model when $u_t = 0$ and there is no underlying drift in the inflation rate. If the random term u_t is identically zero, the observed price level p_t equals the underlying price level $\bar{p}_t$ and the actual observed inflation rate will equal $\bar{p}_t - \bar{p}_{t-1}$. Thus, the second equation, (2.13) becomes (2.1). Similarly, (2.14) is the same as (2.2) when the $\bar{d}_t$ is dropped.

The corresponding forecasting procedure that Jacobs and Jones use is a three-level adaptive-learning rule:

$$\hat{p}_{t+1} = \hat{p}_t + \lambda_1(p_t - \hat{p}_t) + \hat{y}_{t+1} \qquad (2.16)$$

$$\hat{y}_{t+1} = \hat{y}_t + \lambda_2(p_t - \hat{p}_t) + \hat{d}_{t+1} \qquad (2.17)$$

$$\hat{d}_{t+1} = \hat{d}_t + \lambda_3(p_t - \hat{p}_t) \qquad (2.18)$$

If there is an error in forecasting prices, $(p_t - \hat{p}_t) \neq 0$, then the expected drift is revised by some fraction of the error. There are similar revisions in the expected inflation rate and the expected price level.

Using price data from 1947 to 1975, Jacobs and Jones generate price forecasts on the basis of values for λ_1, λ_2, λ_3, and, in effect, select values that yield forecasts whose differences from the consensus Livingston forecasts are as small as possible in terms of a minimum-squared-deviation criterion they select.

They then conduct tests by imposing various restrictions on the forecasting model and seeing whether these restrictions significantly raise the squared deviations between the $\hat{p}_t$ terms generated by their model and the consensus forecasts in the Livingston survey. It turns out that the drift term is not important. Imposing the restriction $\lambda_3 = 0$ does not alter the squared deviations significantly.

When $\lambda_1 = 1$, equation (2.16) becomes an identity, since the expected rate of inflation $\hat{y}_{t+1}$ is defined as $\hat{p}_{t+1} - p_t$. A test of this restriction amounts to a test of whether the forecasters act as if they observe the underlying price level precisely or with some error. Jacobs and Jones reject the hypothesis $\lambda_1 = 1$ in favor of $\lambda_1 > 1$. The estimated value is about 1.2. They interpret this as indicating that the forecasters are not even sure about the underlying price level, let alone the underlying inflation rate.

The view that the forecasters are not sure of the price level is reinforced by the results of another test. When the Livingston surveys are returned in early June or December, the May or November CPI has not been reported, but the forecasters have observed some prices in those months. Jacobs and Jones find that the model better explains the consensus forecasts when they use the May or November CPI as the most recent information rather than the April or October CPI, which would be the latest officially reported values. Individual experiences and perceptions, other than of the CPI series itself, apparently influence the experts as well as respondents to household surveys.

Finally, Jacobs and Jones test whether there might have been a marked break in the early 1960s in the way forecasts were related to prices, a result Turnovsky (1970) claimed to have found. By considering the periods 1947-1961 and 1961-1975 separately, they did get different estimates for λ_1 and λ_2 but no significant reduction in squared deviations compared with using one set of parameter values for the whole 1947-1975 period. The differences are that λ_1 was closer to 1 and λ_2 was much larger in the 1961-1975 period. Presumably, this means that forecasters have become more aware of the actual price level and their inflation forecasts have become more responsive to price forecasting errors.

Jacobs and Jones do not run comparable experiments with the actual values of the CPI being forecast, so we do not know how different the coefficients would be from those that best explained the forecasts. One clue can be gleaned from their test of $\lambda_1 = 1$. In that case, they have an estimate of about .10 for λ_2. If we ignore the small drift term, this value for λ_2 is equivalent to $\theta = .90$ in the Muth model discussed in Section 5. From equation (2.5), $\theta = .9$ when $g = .01$. This means that the variance of the transitory shifts σ_v^2 is perceived to be about 100 times as large as the variance of the permanent shifts σ_w^2, or the ratio of their standard deviations is about ten to one.

Clearly, the Livingston forecasters are slower to perceive permanent shocks to the inflation rate than time-series analysis suggests that they should be. With time-series analysis, Pearce found $\theta = .73$. In terms of adaptive forecasts, equation (2.6), a value of $\theta = .73$ calls for inflation forecasts to be adjusted each month by about one-fourth of the last error, while the Jacobs and Jones estimates (ignoring the price perception problem) indicate that the Livingston consensus forecasts tend to adjust by about one-tenth of the forecasting error each month.

Such results are consistent with what psychologists working in Bayesian research have labeled "conservatism." In a survey article, Slovic and Lichtenstein write: "Upon receipt of new information, subjects revise their posterior probability estimates in the same direction as the optimal model, but the revision is typically *too small*...." They cite research in which "subjects require from two to nine data observations to revise their opinions as much as Bayes' theorem would prescribe for one observation (1971, p. 693)."

Pearce used his time-series estimates of equation (2.11) to develop a two-pronged critique of the Livingston forecasts. The first point was that the time-series forecasts are considerably more accurate, primarily because they do not underestimate inflation as much nor as extensively as the Livingston forecasts during the period from 1960 to 1975. Taking a rational expectations view of the world, Pearce suggests that since the forecasters could have known the relationships he estimated, their forecasts should have done at least as well. The implication is that either the respondents did not believe their own forecasts or they are not representative of truly informed opinion about the inflation process.

There are reasons to be suspicious of this argument. Why should the forecasters have used that particular formula in the 1960s and early 1970s? If we take Nelson's time-series model of inflation, published in 1972, the suggestion is that into the mid-1960s inflation tended to gravitate back to about 2 percent. We know that perceptions and expectations of inflation are influenced by personal experience, often over a lifetime, and in some cases by considerations of history preceding one's lifetime. It is perfectly believable that even informed observers may take years to become convinced that most upward blips in the inflation rate signal a permanently higher inflation. Research by psychologists supports this view.

Pearce's other point challenges the representativeness of the Livingston forecasters of traders in Treasury bill markets and financial markets in general. He begins by assuming the following equation holds:

$$i_t = b_0 + b_1 p_t^e + u_t \qquad (2.19)$$

where i_t is an interest rate on Treasury bills at time t, p_t^e is the expected rate of inflation over the term to maturity of the bill, u_t is a random error, and b_0 and b_1 are constants to be estimated. When the equation is estimated with semiannual observations from 1959-1975, the fit is notably better when the time-series forecasts of expected inflation are used instead of the Livingston series. Furthermore, when both expected inflation series are put into the same regression, time-series data remain statistically significant and the Livingston forecasts do not. According to Pearce, this tells us that all the relevant information in the Livingston forecasts is contained in the time-series forecasts.

These results are an important warning that many studies using the Livingston inflation forecasts may have been mistaken in assuming that they represented views of market traders. At the same time, we should not accept the time-series forecasts either until a number of questions are explored more fully.

Why do the time-series data perform better in this regression? Is the equation too simple, so that the time-series forecasts are statistically capturing effects that are not intended by the theory? Is it because of a few extreme observations or is the fit better most of the time? If "the market" believed these time-series forecasts, why were these beliefs not conveyed to the experts Livingston surveyed? Can we find a subset of the experts whose forecasts worked as well as the time-series forecasts?

If the market participants expected inflation to proceed in accordance with these time-series forecasts, were their expected real returns (interest rate minus expected inflation) consistent with a prudent investment strategy? As one example, at the end of 1974, one-year U.S. Treasury bills were yielding 7.2 percent. According to Pearce's time-series forecasts, "the market" was expecting an annual inflation rate of about 11.4 percent. Thus, the inference is that a buyer of a Treasury bill was expecting a real loss of about 4.2 percent. If these were "rational expectations," as Pearce calls them, what prevented marginal investors from switching into items that were expected to appreciate by at least 11.4 percent and thereby driving up Treasury bill rates accordingly?

These and many other questions need to be answered before economists will know much about which views of expected inflation are relevant to interest rate determination, but the existence of expectations data makes such an investigation possible.

We return once more to the issue of rational expectations. Is it a an effective working hypothesis to assume that people on average make unbiased forecasts of economic variables that will affect how well off they will be in the future?[6] Our concern at the moment is not how to get rational expectations solutions to models or whether certain propositions hold when rational expectations are assumed. Rather, it is a more fundamental question of whether we should rule out on a priori grounds a type of "irrationality" that may characterize people's perceptions of the economy.

---

6. Shiller (1978) provides a thorough survey and critique of technical issues surrounding rational expectations models.

To put the question into a specific framework, consider the problem in the manufacture of most consumer goods. The decisions to acquire materials, hire labor, and undertake a volume of production require forecasts of demand well in advance of actual sales. The prices at which the goods come on the market may also have to be decided in advance. The conglomeration of thousands, perhaps millions, of projections of future demands and future prices that go into wage negotiating, price setting, and production scheduling may not be consistent with the eventual employment and prices that materialize.

Rational expectations advocates ask us to assume that the forecasts are correct on average. That may or may not be true, but it is something that should be tested rather than assumed. The downward bias in the Livingston forecasts is not consistent with that assumption.

Other tests can be made. One concerns the timing of changes in output and employment relative to when errors in forecasting inflation occur. Rational expectations models, such as the one by Lucas (1973), predict that an unexpected burst of inflation is concurrent with or comes before an increase in output and employment.

As an alternative to the rational expectations prediction, it can be shown that when firms are overly optimistic about the level of demand or when labor commands unrealistic wage expectations, prices will be higher than expected. If the real-wage expectations respond with a lag to employment conditions, then we could find that price-forecasting errors are greatest well after employment has peaked and become accurate again only after the economy has gone into a recession. The prediction here is that unexpected inflation becomes large after employment has reached high levels.

Evidence reported by Carlson (1980) supports this latter prediction. The strongest association between the percent of the population employed and the errors made by the Livingston forecasters in predicting inflation occur when the employment variable precedes the time of the forecast by six months and the eventual revealed errors by a full year. Similar timing holds for implicit forecasts of inflation in interest rate data. These results should warn us not to assume away a consistent inability to predict inflation during and immediately following periods of high employment.

There is a subtle issue here. Advocates of rational expectations argue that if people had used a particular model of the inflation process they would have made better forecasts than survey data tell us they did. Therefore, the argument goes, it would not be in people's self-interest to ignore the information in this model, and since it is postulated that people behave in their own self-interest, one should not believe the survey results. The alternative argument is that it takes a long time and a great deal of convincing evidence, like regular tides, before people will generally agree on the same model. In using diverse models and bits of information, people may well on average make systematic errors. In that case, the rational expectations approach is assuming away what people actually do.

Pearce's other way of comparing survey measures and time-series forecasts in terms of goodness-of-fit statistics in an interest-rate equation, while in need of a more thorough investigation, is a more telling criticism. For one thing, it highlights something we already know from the survey data: different people with different experiences have different expectations. Therefore, one should not take the mean forecast from a highly selective survey and assume unquestioningly that it represents the expectations of any group of people. The same challenge, of course, applies to users of time-series forecasts. Why should a model selected and estimated by a single researcher represent the expectations of any particular group of economic agents?

7. Concluding Remarks

In the United States in recent years we have seen a pattern of inflation rising during a boom in economic activity and then coming down during or immediately following a recession to troughs that have been higher after each successive recession. This pattern can be seen in annual rates of change of a general price index, such as the CPI, but these changes do not proceed smoothly. Relative prices often change substantially, and transitory changes dominate the monthly inflation rates in the CPI. This is what most people see, without much of an overall perspective. They may know that the prices of specific items are being changed from time to time and they surely become aware that price increases are eroding the purchasing power of their money. Still, there are substantial differences in awareness of how quickly these prices are rising on average.

At the outset, we asked what is meant by the expected rate of inflation. In our emphasis on the difficulties in discriminating between permanent and transitory changes or between relative and general price changes and on the different models, perceptions, and expectations, we may have created the impression that expectations of inflation are so diverse that they do not really matter. If so, we would like to dispel that notion. What we mean to stress is that expected inflation is not easily measured.

The evidence reviewed here does warrant the following general statement. Inflation will be expected to be higher when, other things being equal, inflation itself has been higher in the recent past. This is because perceptions of inflation are related to actual experience and observation, and expectations appear to vary systematically with perceptions even though opinions may be dispersed and different measures of expected inflation will have different values at a particular time.

We are not in a position to make categorical statements about how important inflation expectations are in the inflation process. This is because we do not have good evidence of precisely how this works, how actual behavior is related to stated expectations or to what advocates of time-series forecasts say people's expectations were or should have been. As competing measures of expectations and alternative hypotheses are put forward, systematic tests can be conducted. That literature is still very much in its infancy.

References

Box, George E. P., and G. M., Jenkins. 1970. *Time Series Analysis: Forecasting and Control.* San Franciso: Holden-Day.

Carlson, John A. 1975. "Are Price Expectations Normally Distributed?" *Journal of the American Statistical Association* 70 (December), pp. 749-754.

Carlson, John A. 1977. "A Study of Price Forecasts." *Annals of Economic and Social Measurement* 6 (Winter), pp. 27-56.

Carlson, John A. 1980. "Systematic Errors in Inflation Forecasts." In W. H. Strigel *Business Cycle Analysis*, Gower Publishing Co., pp. 117-141.

Carlson, John A., and M. Parkin. 1975. "Inflation Expectations." *Economica* 42 (May), pp. 123-138.

Cukierman, Alex. 1979. "The Relationship between Relative Prices and the General Price Level: A Suggested Interpretation." *American Economic Review* 69 (June), pp. 444-447.

Cukierman, A., and P. Wachtel. 1979. "Differential Inflationary

Expectations and the Variability of the Rate of Inflation: Theory and Evidence." *American Economic Review* 69 (September), pp. 595-609.

Danes, M. 1975. "The Measurement and Explanation of Inflationary Expectations in Australia." *Australian Economic Papers* 14 (June), pp. 75-87.

Defris, L. V., and R. A. Williams. 1979. "The Formation of Consumer Inflationary Expectations in Australia." *Economic Record* 55 (June), pp. 136-148.

DeMenil, G., and S. S. Bhalla. 1975. "Direct Measures of Popular Price Expectations." *American Economic Review* 65 (March), pp. 169-180.

Fama, Eugene F. 1970. "Efficient Capital Markets: A Review of Theory and Empirical Work." *Journal of Finance* 25 (May), pp. 383-417.

Foster, E. 1979. "The Variability of Inflation." *Review of Economics and Statistics* 60 (August), pp. 346-350.

Gale, William A. 1981. "Temporal Variability of United States Consumer Price Index." *Journal of Money, Credit and Banking,* forthcoming.

Glejser, H. 1965. "Inflation, Productivity, and Relative Prices — A Statistical Study." *Review of Economics and Statistics* 47 (February), pp. 76-80.

Gordon, R. J. 1971. "Steady Anticipated Inflation: Mirage or Oasis." *Brookings Papers on Economic Activity* No. 2, pp. 499-510.

Hogg, R. V., and A. T. Craig. 1970. *Introduction to Mathematical Statistics,* 3rd ed. London: Macmillan.

Jacobs, R. L., and R. A. Jones. 1980. "Price Expectations in the United States: 1947-75." *American Economic Review* 70 (June), pp. 269-277.

Jonung, Lars. 1980. "Perceived and Expected Rates of Inflation. A Note on Sweden," *American Economic Review,* forthcoming.

Juster, F. T., and R. Comment. 1978. "A Note on the Measurement of Price Expectations." Unpublished, University of Michigan.

Logue, D. E., and T. D. Willett. 1976. "A Note on the Relation between the Rate and Variability of Inflation." *Economica* 43 (May), pp. 151-158.

Lucas, R. E. Jr. 1972. "Econometric Testing of the Natural Rate Hypothesis." *Conference on the Econometrics of Price Determination.* Washington, D.C., pp. 50-59.

Lucas, R. E. Jr. 1973. "Some International Evidence on Output-Inflation Tradeoffs." *American Economic Review* 63 (June), pp. 326-334.

Lucas, R. E. Jr. 1976. "Econometric Policy Evaluation: A Critique." In K. Brunner and A. Meltzer, ed., *The Phillips Curve and Labor Markets* (Amsterdam), pp. 19-46. (Supplement to the *Journal of Monetary Economics*).

Michael, Robert T. 1979. "Variation Across Households in the Rate of Inflation." *Journal of Money, Credit and Banking* 11 (February), pp. 32-46.

Mills, F. C. 1927. *The Behavior of Prices.* New York: National Bureau of Economic Research.

Mullineaux, D. J. 1978. "More on the Rationality of the Livingston Price Expectations." *Journal of Political Economy* 86 (April), pp. 329-336.

Mullineaux, D. J. 1980. "Inflation Expectations and Money Growth in the United States." *American Economic Review* 70 (March), pp. 149-161.

Muth, John F. 1960. "Optimal Properties of Exponentially Weighted Forecasts." *Journal of American Statistical Association* 55 (June), pp. 299-306.

Muth, John F. 1961. "Rational Expectations and the Theory of Price Movements." *Econometrica* 29 (July), pp. 315-335.

Nelson, Charles R. 1972. "The Predictive Performance of the FRB-MIT-PENN Model of the U.S. Economy." *American Economic Review* 62 (December), pp. 902-917.

Okun, Arthur. 1971. "The Mirage of Steady Inflation." *Brookings Papers on Economic Activity* No. 2, pp. 485-498.

Parks, R. W. 1978. "Inflation and Relative Price Variability." *Journal of Political Economy* 86 (February), pp. 79-96.

Pearce, Douglas K. 1979. "Comparing Survey and Rational Measures of Expected Inflation." *Journal of Money, Credit and Banking* 11 (November), pp. 447-456.

Pesando, J. 1975. "A Note on Rationality of the Livingston Price Expectations Data." *Journal of Political Economy* 83 (August), pp. 849-854.

Sargent, T. J. 1973. "Rational Expectations, the Real Rate of Interest and the Natural Rate of Unemployment." *Brookings Papers on Economic Activity* No. 2, pp. 429-472.

Schultze, Charles. 1959. "Recent Inflation in the U.S." Study paper no. 1 for the Joint Economic Committee, Washington, D.C.

Shiller, R. J. 1978. "Rational Expectations and the Dynamic Structure of Macroeconomic Models." *Journal of Monetary Economics* 4 (January), pp. 1-44.

Sims, C. A. 1974. "Distributed Lags." In M. Intriligator and D. Kendrick, eds., *Frontiers of Quantitative Economics*, Vol. II. Amsterdam, pp. 289-332.

Slovic, P., and S. Lichtenstein. 1971. "Comparison of Bayesian and Regression Approaches to the Study of Information Processing in Judgment." *Organizational Behavior and Human Performance* 6 (November), pp. 649-744.

Solow, Robert. 1975. "The Intelligent Citizen's Guide to Inflation." *Public Interest*, 38 (Winter), pp. 30-66.

Solow, Robert. 1980. "What to Do (Macroeconomically) When OPEC

Comes." In Stanley Fisher, ed., *Rational Expectations and Economic Policy*, University of Chicago Press, pp. 249-264.

Tversky, A., and D. Kahneman. 1974. "Judgment under Uncertainty: Heuristics and Biases." *Science* 185 (September), pp. 1124-1131.

Turnovsky, S. J. 1970. "Empirical Evidence on the Formation of Price Expectations." *Journal of the American Statistical Association* 65 (December), pp. 1441-1154.

Wachtel, Paul. 1977. "Survey Measures of Expected Inflation and Their Potential Usefulness." in J. Popkin (ed.), *Analysis of Inflation 1965-74*, NBER Studies in Income and Wealth, pp. 361-395.

Vining, D. R., Jr., and T. C. Elwertowski. 1976. "The Relationship Between Relative Prices and the General Price Level." *American Economic Review* 66 (September), pp. 699-708.

3

How Well Can We Measure Price Changes?

William A. Gale

Bell Telephone Laboratories

1. Introduction

How well we can measure price changes limits our ability to see many economic phenomena through time series analysis. Economic theory says that to compare across time we need real(constant dollar) rather than nominal (current dollar) monetary units. So any time series study using quantities measured in nominal monetary units needs to adjust them to real units. In practice, we divide a series in nominal monetary units by a comprehensive price index, called a deflator. Its accuracy limits our ability to deflate, and hence to know.

Many time series methods may be affected by errors in a deflator, but this study restricts attention to the effect in regression. Errors in a series bias a regression-estimated coefficient for that series. We look at the regression of a series measured without error on one other series that has only deflator errors. The bias in the coefficient for the deflated series is used to compare various errors in using the U.S. Consumer Price Index (CPI) as a deflator, and to assess their combined effect.

The CPI is widely used for deflation in econometric work. Compiled by the Bureau of Labor Statistics, it summarizes information about prices paid by consumers. It had its origin in 1917 for use in wage adjustments. This is still a major use of the CPI, which now covers about 6 million workers and those on social security. The index is designed to measure price changes, not absolute price levels. It uses fixed weights, adding to unity, in forming an average of observed price changes. The weights used are the fraction of household budgets spent on the goods represented, as determined by the Survey of Consumer Expenditure. The CPI has been revised and expanded approximately every ten years. At such times the weights are changed to reflect usage changes. The most recent revisions were effective in January 1978, 1964, and 1953.

The errors discussed here are those that result from using the CPI for a given econometric purpose. There may be other errors, or other impacts of the same errors, for different purposes. Since an error can only be defined with respect to a purpose, there can be no error, per se, in the compilation of the CPI except a failure to describe the process accurately. Understanding an econometric purpose as implied, we will speak of "errors." We compare the effects from the following errors: (1) consistent omission of some goods, (2) omission of consumers in determining the weights for the goods, (3) periodic omission of some goods, (4) not allowing for the substitution of goods when their relative prices change, (5) not allowing for changes over time in consumer preferences, (6) incomplete measurement of quality changes, and (7) sampling errors. We find that for series used for annual regressions, the worst problems are omitted goods and quality changes. For quarterly series, these are surpassed by omitted consumers. For monthly series, quality changes are the worst problem. This is part of the information needed to determine where future resources for measuring prices should be put. The other part is estimating how expensive the improvement of any particular error would be, which is not covered here.

The errors considered here are assumed to be unbiased. This is an optimistic assumption. However, bias has long been examined, and has been difficult to establish without making a better measurement. Once a better measurement has been made, it is fairly easy to incorporate the method into the standard procedures. Then the revised procedures no longer give an index known to be biased. Thus the worst case can be specified as a deflator with the same variance in its changes as the CPI, but for which the changes are purely random, having nothing to do with prices. This would be called unbiased noise.

This paper shows that in some cases, especially when the nominal price changes have a much larger variance than the CPI changes, even a deflator that was unbiased noise would be of little importance. However, when the nominal price series is such that the deflator is important, the errors that arise from using the CPI for deflation are significant. For a regression using monthly data, the bias in the coefficient for the deflated variable can be about 2.9. That is, the estimated coefficient can be biased toward zero by a factor of about 2.9. For quarterly and yearly data, the corresponding biases can be 1.67 and 1.07 . Thus it is our result that we can measure annual price changes fairly well, quarterly price changes poorly, and monthly price changes essentially not at all.

Analysts have two ways of coping with the deflator errors described here. First, they can select as long a time period as possible consistent with their analysis. Second, they can make a correction to the biased coefficients, as discussed in Section 5. For if the errors are known exactly, so is the bias, and they can multiply the biased coefficients by the bias. Unfortunately, errors are not known exactly, so uncertainty remains after correcting. Correction leaves uncertainty of 2 percent, 20 percent, and 30 percent for coefficients of annual, quarterly, and monthly series.

While the paper is focuses on the CPI, most of the errors would have counterparts if the Producer Price Index, or Gross National Product Deflator (GNPD), were used. The concept differences quantified are coverage of goods, coverage of consumers, time period mismatches, goods substitution, dynamic concepts, quality adjustment, and sampling. Section 2 describes the criterion in more detail, and the third section briefly reviews each of the differences quantified. The differences are then compared.

2. Criterion

This section develops a criterion for comparing errors in a deflator. To do so it discusses the effect of deflator error in simple regressions. (Appendix A contains the bulk of the algebra, although a simple discussion is presented in this section.) First, some definitions. Let P_t, D_t, and Q_t represent respectively the logarithms of the nominal price for some good, a deflator, and a directly measured quantity of the good. Denote by p_t, d_t, and q_t the first differences of the corresponding variables denoted by upper case letters. Then the regression used as the "criterion" regression is

$$q_t = a_1 + b_1(p_t - d_t) + u_t$$

where the u_t are independently normally distributed with mean zero and constant variance. Although phrased as a demand model, the results depend only on the structure of the model and not on its interpretation. The key assumptions of the model are that p_t is measured in nominal monetary units, without error, and that q_t is measured in real units.

The criterion regression is quite simple even compared to the ordinary one commodity demand equation in that it lacks terms for income, lagged dependent variable, seasonality, and specific discrete events that are often present in such an equation. While it is possible to state the effect of deflator error in such extended models, the results will depend on a large number of facts that vary from one equation to another. For a criterion, it is better to focus attention on the deflator. Also, the comparison of the magnitudes of the individual errors does not need a complex setting. This equation does allow for the first order effect of interaction between the nominal price and deflator.

A first difference model is used, not because that is usual practice, but because the bias in the coefficient b_1 is equivalent to the bias in the coefficient b_2 in

$$Q_t = a_2 + b_2(P_t - D_t)$$

when the means of the nominal price changes and the deflator changes are equal. This is proved in Appendix B. It is also equivalent to the bias in the coefficient b_3 of

$$Q_t = a_3 + b_3(P_t - D_t) + c_3 t$$

because the time term absorbs the information from any drift between nominal price and deflator. In common econometric practice, terms such as income with a strong time trend are present; the equation is a simple model of the more realistic situation. In the sequel, there is no use of the absolute quantities, and references to "price" may be used instead of the full reference to "price changes."

According to standard errors-in-variable theory (Johnston, 1972), the asymptotic expected value of b_1 will be biased toward zero if the errors in measuring the real price changes $p_t - d_t$ are unbiased and uncorrelated with the true values. Since we are considering only errors in the deflator, and since we can reasonably expect that the errors made will be correlated with the true deflator, Appendix A (Section A.2) considers the following model of the effect of an error of omission in the deflator. The true deflator is given by

$$d_t = (1-f)w_t + fy_t$$

However, only the portion w_t of the deflator is known, and the portion y_t is omitted. The bias in b_1 depends on f, the fraction omitted, on

$\tau \equiv$ standard deviation(p_t)/standard deviation(d_t)

$\rho_{pw} \equiv$ correlation between p_t and w_t

$\rho_{py} \equiv$ correlation between p_t and y_t

and on

$\rho_{wy} \equiv$ correlation between w_t and y_t

With standard Ordinary Least Squares assumptions about the estimation of b_1, then the asymptotic expected ratio

$$plim\,(\hat{b}_1)/b_1 = 1 - f(1-\rho_{wy})/(\tau^2 - 2\rho_{pw}\tau + 1)$$

In the derivation in Appendix Sections A.1 and A.2, it is pointed out that the quantities ρ_{pw} and ρ_{py} enter only as their difference. Since only model-dependent assumptions determined the sign of this difference, it was assumed to be zero for the purpose of developing a criterion.

Figures 3.1 and 3.2 show the result for omission errors graphically. The plots show the *fractional error*, defined by

$$\phi = \frac{plim\,(\hat{b}_1) - b_1}{b}$$

Figure 3.1 plots the fractional error for omission as a function of f and ρ_{wy} for $\tau = 1$ and $\rho_{pw} = .5$. It shows that for nothing omitted ($f = 0$) or perfect correlation between the omitted and included portions ($\rho_{wy} = 1$), then there is no error. The fractional error goes to -1 as both $f \rightarrow 1$ and $\rho_{wy} \rightarrow 0$. Figure 3.2 shows the fractional error as a function of τ and $\tau\rho_{pw}$ for $f = .25$ and $\rho_{wy} = .5$. It shows the decline of the bias factor as τ increases and the increase of the bias factor with increasing ρ_{pw}. Table 3.1 shows some example values for τ and ρ_{pw} from modeling telephone demand for τ and ρ_{pw}. It also includes a set of entries based on the major commodities discussed later.

Another representation of the results here is by an equivalent signal-to-noise ratio. The equivalence is to the strength of the noise signal, which, if uncorrelated with the true price, would give the calculated fractional error for a regression on real price. Equation 9-43 of Johnston (1972) gives

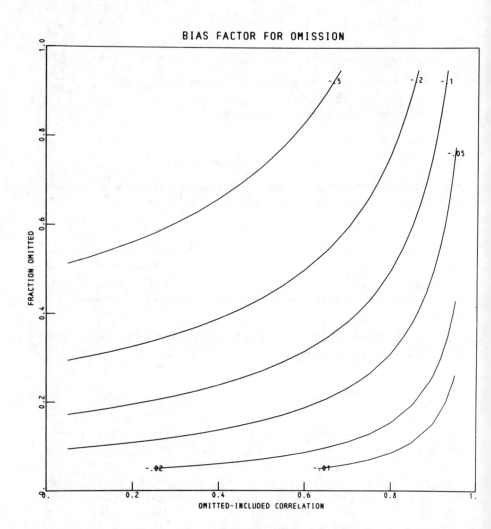

Figure 3.1
Bias Factor for Omission
as a Function of Omitted-Included Correlation

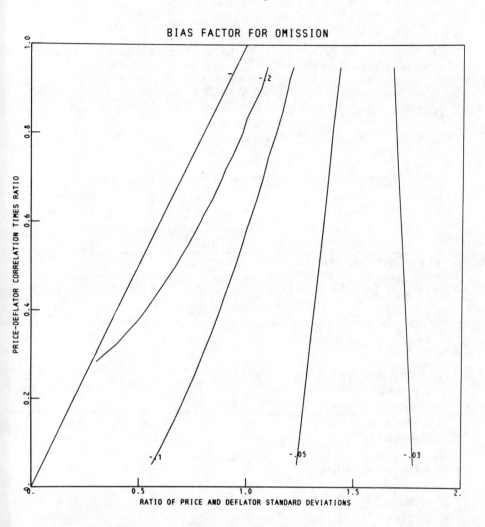

Figure 3.2
Bias Factor for Omission as a Function of Standard Deviations

$$plim\,(\hat{b}_1)/b_1 = 1/(1+N/S)$$

for noise and signal variances N and S. For an equivalent signal to noise ratio, we identify

$$1/(1+N/S) = 1 + \phi$$

giving

$$S/N = (1+\phi)/-\phi$$

Table 3.1
Example Relationships Between Nominal Price and CPI

Nominal Price	Ratio of Price and Deflator Standard Deviations (τ)	Price-Deflator Correlation (ρ_{pw})
Long-distance, state A		
monthly	9.1	.10
quarterly	6.7	.15
yearly	3.5	.40
Long-distance, state B	.0	.00
Long-distance, all intrastate		
monthly	2.4	.35
quarterly	1.4	.60
yearly	1.3	.75
median of		
Major commodities		
monthly	1	.21
quarterly	1	.50
yearly	1	.84

The first two examples in Table 3.1 are the long-distance intrastate service in two particular states. In state A, there have been eight price changes in the last sixteen years. The average price increase over the sixteen years was 73 percent of the average CPI increase over the period. Since the telephone price changes were concentrated into just a few nonzero changes (because of the regulatory process), τ is large. The price-deflator correlations are surprisingly large even here. Notice that for state A, τ declines with increasing period and ρ_{pw} increases. In state B, there were no long-distance price changes during the last ten years. Accordingly both τ and ρ_{pw} are zero. It would of course be foolish to attempt a demand analysis with such facts. The example is included to indicate that the other states could be expected to lie between these two cases. The third and fourth examples show the effect of studying an aggregate commodity. The third example is all intrastate long-distance telephone service. The fourth shows the median values for five very aggregate commodities such as food and housing. In these two examples, the values for τ are distinctly lower than those for state A, and the price-deflator correlations are distinctly higher.

The effects of deflator errors will be shown for these examples, but because they show variation of τ and ρ_{pw} by time period, we also define "criterion" values of $\tau = 1$ and $\rho_{pw} = .5$. These values are included in the range of values in Table 3.1. This will allow us to compare the effects of errors for differing time periods without varying the effect of price-deflator interaction. The criterion values will be implicit in a reference to "criterion regression."

For the criterion regression, as for more complex regressions, a first-order correction can be made to give an unbiased estimator if the amount of the bias is known. For the criterion regression, the correction is simply to multiply the estimated coefficient (but not its estimated standard deviation) by the reciprocal of one plus the fractional error. If the sources of error can be exactly characterized statistically, there is no remaining bias in the resulting estimator. In the estimates developed later, there is some uncertainty in the amount of the bias factor, which translates into an additional variance term even for an adjusted coefficient.

3. Discussion of Errors

This section discusses the basis for quantifying errors due to omitted goods, omitted consumers, time period mismatches, substitution of goods, dynamic effects, quality adjustments, and sampling. Some errors not quantified are mentioned in Section 4.

3.1 Omitted Goods

Table 3.2 shows estimates of the amount of goods omitted from the CPI. The first line of the table shows no omission for government-purchased goods and services. This is correct for demand analysis if the following assumptions hold: (1) The consumers' decisions about consumer goods and government goods are *separable,* that is, the decisions about what consumer goods to buy are based only on how much money is available for those goods, and not on how much was spent or what was bought through the government. (2) The consumers buy items with sales or property taxes using *individual* rationality, assuming that the tax benefits to themselves from their own sales taxes are negligible. (3) The income used is disposable personal income *plus* sales and property taxes, (which we shall call "allocable" income). The amounts in Table 3.2 are shown as fractions of allocable income. Under other assumptions, or for other problems, there may be severe omission problems from this source, because government provided goods and services account for 21 percent of the GNP.

The second line of Table 3.2 shows that an estimated 4 percent of allocable income is spent on goods that by design are not included in the CPI. The Bureau of Labor Statistics (BLS) recognizes two categories of deliberately omitted goods, "out of scope" and "truncated." Out-of-scope goods include work expenses such as union dues, professional society dues, and commuting expenses. It also includes some goods, such as life insurance, which the BLS has been unable to decide how to measure. Out-of-scope goods are not included in the Consumer Expenditure Survey (CES). Truncated goods are included, but not in the population from which the goods actually priced are sampled. These include religious and charitable contributions, primary and secondary private schooling, foreign travel, and vehicles other than autos such as trucks, motorcycles, and airplanes. The estimate of 4 percent is based on comparing the Table 2.6 of the July 1977 Survey of Current Business (Personal Consumption Expenditures by Type of Expenditure) with the described omissions.

The third line of the table estimates that 5 percent of allocable income is spent on goods that are too new to be included in the most recent CES. This has long been noted as a possible source of bias (Rees, 1961), because new goods typically are falling rapidly in price. No estimate has been made of the magnitude of the bias, and no correction is made. A current example of a new good is the smoke detector. For another example, until sales of color televisions became equal to those of black-and-white televisions, color TVs were not included in the CPI. The estimate of 5 percent is very crudely based on the previously mentioned Table 2.6 of the Survey of Current Business. It was assumed that all percentage increases in the categories of that table from one year to another were due to new goods and that only such increases were for new goods. The changes were taken for one through ten years, and averaged.

The final line of the table shows 8 percent of allocable income spent for "moonlight" goods and services. This includes not only goods and services that are per se illegal, but also the much larger markets conducted in cash to avoid income tax. Peter Gutmann (1977) has estimated the size of the monetary moonlight market as 10 percent of GNP. Government estimates have not been published, but they would presumably be smaller. Some of these goods will be captured in the CES, but they will not be priced, and thus are omitted from the price index.

Table 3.2
Percentages of Omitted Goods

Government provided goods and services	0%
Omitted by design	4
New goods	5
Moonlight goods and services	8
Total	17

The previous remarks explain the basis for estimating the fraction of goods omitted. We also need an estimate of the correlation between the price changes for both omitted and included goods. Since the prices for the omitted goods are difficult to observe, or even hard to define, we cannot calculate this estimate directly. However, the BLS publishes the CPI by goods categories. Knowing the correlation between a major goods category, such as food, and the remainder of the index gives a basis for estimating other omitted-included correlations. We can calculate five different correlations between an omitted category and the remainder of the index using the major goods categories: food, housing, apparel, transportation, and medical-personal. These give a range within which a high or low estimate of the correlations for the goods actually omitted may lie. This is of course an assumption, not a guarantee.

Figures 3.3 through 3.5 give a visual impression of the results. They show scatter plots for the inflation rates measured by the apparel index and by the index of all goods except apparel. Apparel was selected for display because its correlations were the median correlations among the five major commodities. Figure 3.3, monthly price changes, shows very little relation. Figure 3.4, quarterly price changes, shows some relation, with an absence of points in the upper left and lower right. Figure 3.5, annual price changes, shows a fairly strong relation. Thus, if apparel were omitted from the index for some reason, we would have considerably less error in annual measurements than in monthly measurements.

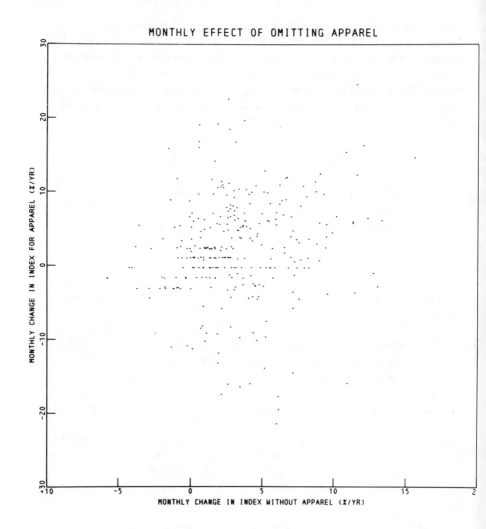

Figure 3.3
Monthly Effect of Omitting Apparel

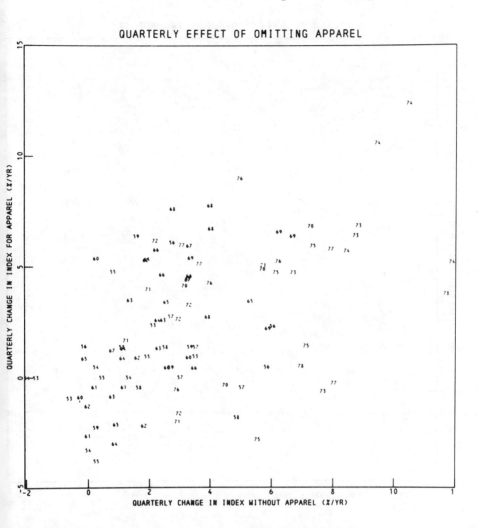

Figure 3.4
Quarterly Effect of Omitting Apparel

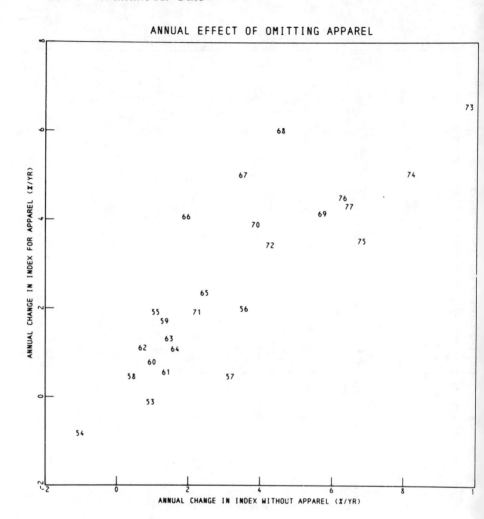

Figure 3.5
Annual Effect of Omitting Apparel

Table 3.3 shows the correlations for omission of each major goods category, based on the CPI from June 1953 through June 1978, a total of 300 months. In each case, the series of remaining goods is calculated with the usage weights. The table shows correlations for three periods — monthly, quarterly, and yearly. It also shows correlations calculated with equal weights and bisquare weights. The bisquare weights, described in the next paragraph, give reduced weight to points that lie far from the bulk of the points. They give an estimate based on the main part of the data, which is probably a better basis for analogy with unmeasured goods. In this case, the differences between equal weights and bisquare weights are small, but this is not so in all cases. Notice that all the correlations increase as the time period increases. This means that less error will be made for the longer periods.

The bisquare weights used for a location estimate are given by $(1 - u^2)^2$ if $|u| \leq 1$ and 0 otherwise, with $u = (x - m)/ks$, m the median of the values of x, s the median absolute deviation from the median, and $k = 9$. This gives zero weight to observations more than 9 times s from m, and smoothly decreasing weights out to this distance. If a correlation is calculated according to

$$[\text{Var(sum)} - \text{Var(diff)}]/[\text{Var(sum)} + \text{Var(diff)}]$$

where sum and diff are the standardized sum and difference series, then the biweight correlation is calculated with the biweight variance. The biweight variance used is that given by Mosteller and Tukey (1977, p. 208), and weights the differences from the median by the squares of the weighting function above.[1]

---

1. See Devlin et al. (1975) for a discussion of standardized sum and difference correlations.

Table 3.3

Major Commodity Correlations

	Time Period					
	Month		Quarter		Year	
Omitted Good	Equal	Biwt	Equal	Biwt	Equal	Biwt
Food	.06	.01	.34	.29	.72	.71
Housing	.50	.46	.72	.69	.92	.91
Apparel	.14	.20	.50	.51	.84	.88
Transportation	.21	.24	.47	.32	.70	.72
Health-personal	.47	.53	.59	.60	.84	.91
Median	.21	.20	.50	.51	.84	.88

An error related to omission, but treated differently in Appendix Section A.3, is the omission of higher-priced housing from the housing index.[2] The data for the home purchase and finance subindex comes from the Federal Housing Administration (FHA) and refers only to houses with FHA financing. Thus it measures only the price changes for lower priced houses. The amount of the omission is not clear, but this study used 80 percent as a high estimate and 20 percent as a low estimate. The amount of the weight of home purchase and finance in the CPI is 9.1 percent. An additional possible problem with this subindex is that capital appreciation on existing housing is considered only as a cost, and not also as an offsetting income.

3.2 Omitted Consumers

More consumers have been covered with each major revision of the CPI. Table 3.4 shows the omitted consumers since 1953. (The major postwar revisions were in 1953, 1964, and 1978.) For each period between major index changes, the table shows the percentage of the United States population omitted from the CES used. The rural population outside Standard Metropolitan Statistical Areas (SMSAs) has not yet been included. This group has been a continuously declining fraction of the total U.S. population. In 1964, consumers in one-person households were included for the first time. In 1978 the professional-managerial, those on social security and welfare, and the retired were included for the first time. Some small segments that have not yet

2. DeMilner (1978), among others, has cited this problem.

been included are the institutional population, the military, and those living in urban places with population under 2500. The totals of omitted consumers are at the bottom of the table.

For this factor, it is particularly evident that the error structure is not constant over time. Later, the results will be presented for regressions based on 1968-1978 and on 1978-1988. The "1978-1988" designation supposes that current procedures are kept without change for a ten-year period, at the end of which the criterion regression would be performed.

Table 3.4
Omitted Consumers, by Time

	From	1953	1964	1978
	To	1964	1978	—
		%	%	%
Rural outside SMSA		30	26	24
One person household		7	0	0
Professional and unemployed		21	21	0
Institutional		1	1	1
Military		1.5	1.5	1.5
Urban under 2500		.5	.5	.5
Total		61	50	27

We now need to estimate a correlation for the omission of consumers. The CPI is not published by type of consumer; however, it is published by size of city. Since the rural population has been a major omission, examining the effect of a hypothetical omission of customers by city size class will give some idea of the effect of that omission. Figures 3.6 and 3.7 display the scatter plots for the median correlations when city size groups are omitted. Figure 3.6, quarterly price changes, shows a fairly strong relation, while Figure 3.7, annual price changes, shows an extremely strong relation.

Table 3.5 shows the correlations for hypothetically omitted city size classes. Not all size classes are measured every month, as explained in the next section. Thus the table shows only quarterly and yearly periods. The yearly correlations are again higher than the quarterly ones. These correlations are also higher than those for omitted goods.

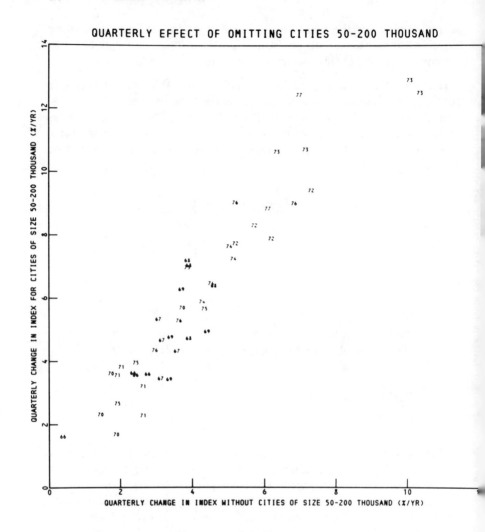

Figure 3.6
Quarterly Effect of Omitting Cites of 50,000 to 200,000

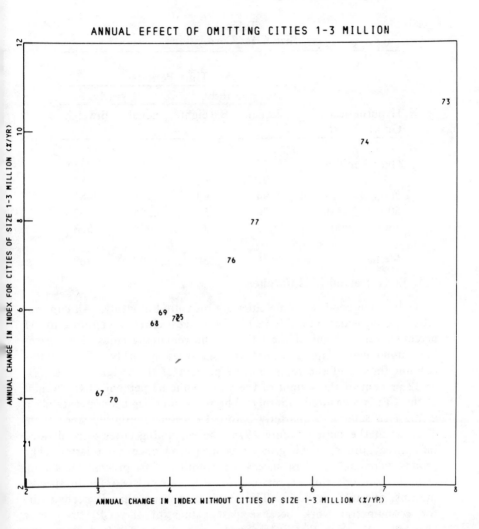

Figure 3.7
Annual Effect of Omitting Cities of 1 Million to 3 Million

Table 3.5
Size Class Correlations

| | Time Periods | | | |
| | quarterly | | yearly | |
Hypothetically Omitted Size	Equal	Biweight	Equal	Biweight
Over 3 million	.49	.39	.958	.925
1-3 million	.91	.88	.990	.989
200,000-1 million	.94	.93	.988	.986
50,000-200,000	.76	.58	.995	.992
2500-50,000	.57	.34	.994	.993
Median	.76	.58	.990	.989

3.3 Time Period Mismatches

Only some goods in some cities are measured monthly. All commodities are measured monthly in the five largest cities, accounting for 31 percent of the weight of the CPI. In the remaining cities, food, gasoline, homeownership, and rent are measured monthly. These items account for .46 of the remaining 69 percent of the weight of the CPI, or 32 percent of the weight of the CPI. Thus 63 percent of the weight of the CPI is measured monthly. The remainder has been measured on a *staggered* schedule, quarterly before 1978 and bimonthly since then. That is, in the period before 1978, the remaining cities were divided into three groups. Each group was measured once per quarter. The groups were measured in successive months. This process creates an error for the criterion regression if the quantity data refer to specific months, quarters, or years. The problem is worse than it needs to be for econometric work because past values of the CPI are never changed. A series that is changed, such as the GNP deflator, can arrange a better match to a given time period.

Table 3.6 shows the effect schematically for a quarterly measurement before 1978. It shows the months and city groups for which measurements are wanted and for which they are available. Each r_{ij} indicates the (unmeasured) price change for all the goods not measured monthly in city j and month i. The figure supposes that each group has equal weight, which is approximately true by design. For the quarter consisting of the months $i = 0,1,2$, the desired measure is $\sum_{j=1}^{3}\sum_{i=0}^{2}r_{ij}$.

But the available data for the quarter is based on measurements made once per quarter in each city group. Thus only six of the desired measurements are available, while three unwanted measurements are included and three desired measurements are excluded. (The measurements excluded from this quarter will appear in the next quarter as unwanted measurements.)

Table 3.6
Quarterly Time Period Mismatch,
Three-month Staggering

	City Group	Month				
		−2	−1	0	1	2
Desired						
	1			$r_{1,0}$	$+r_{1,1}$	$+r_{1,2}$
	2			$+r_{2,0}$	$+r_{2,1}$	$+r_{2,2}$
	3			$+r_{3,0}$	$+r_{3,1}$	$+r_{3,2}$
Available						
	1			$r_{1,0}$	$+r_{1,1}$	$+r_{1,2}$
	2		$+r_{2,-1}$	$+r_{2,0}$	$+r_{2,1}$	
	3	$+r_{3,-2}$	$+r_{3,-1}$	$+r_{3,0}$		

Accounting for this error could give very complicated models. Appendix A develops a relatively simple model, whose empirical basis is set out here. The comparison later suggests that more elaborate models would not be worthwhile, since the effect seems to be small. This work assumes that the correlations between price changes in different groups of cities in different months depend only on the lag between the two months, and on whether the group of cities is the same or different. This model for the autocorrelation and cross correlation structures was derived from the calculations represented in Figure 3.8.

This figure plots the median correlations among the autocorrelations for the five cities measured monthly, and among the ten cross correlations (identifying lags of the same absolute number of months) for the same cities. These median correlations are plotted against the lag in months. The correlations are the biweight correlations. The figure shows that one differencing has not produced a stationary series, since the correlations are falling only very slowly. This is perhaps not surprising for a seasonal series, but it results in less error than if the correlations dropped rapidly to zero. The cross-correlations at positive lags are systematically greater that the autocorrelations, but the difference is not too large compared to the variations in either series.

CORRELATION STRUCTURE BETWEEN CITIES

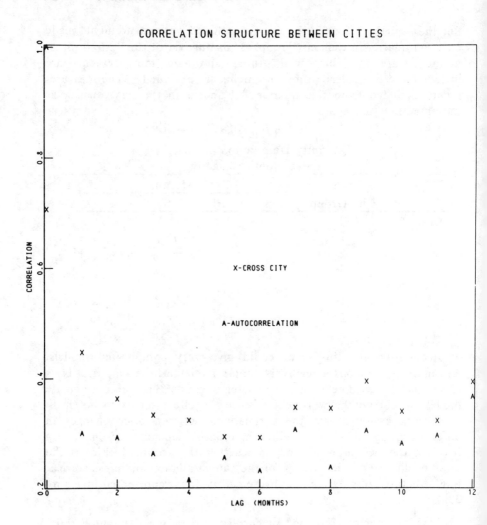

Figure 3.8
Correlation Structure Between Cities

The variations in the series do not appear to be random, because they move up and down together. But these movements and the differences between the auto- and cross-correlations are small enough that they can be put into an uncertainty term rather than be treated individually.

The results in Figure 3.8 were abstracted to the following very simple model. The cross-correlation for price changes in different city groups at zero lag is ω and has low and high values of .65 and .75. The auto- and cross-correlations at all other lags are ρ with low and high values of .25 and .35.

Another factor needed is the correlation between the monthly goods and the nonmonthly goods in different cities as a function of lag. This work assumes that these correlations are independent of city, and of the particular goods. Figure 3.9 shows the median (among five) correlation between each major goods category and all other goods, as a function of lag in months. It is a time extension of the second column of Table 3.3. The nonstationarity is again apparent. This series was modeled by assuming that the first entry was .26, and that all others were .21.

This structure of correlations was used to calculate six submodels, whose results are included in Appendix Section A.5 along with a derivation for one of the submodels.

3.4 Substitution of Goods

When the prices of goods do not all increase together, a consumer can mitigate the effects of rising prices by changing the mix of goods consumed. For example, the price of ground chuck recently increased from roughly the same price as chicken to roughly twice the price for chicken. A consumer could offset the increased price of ground chuck at least in part, by buying less of it and more chicken. The economic concept that quantifies this effect is the cost of living index (COL). The COL index is defined as the ratio of minimum costs to attain the same utility surface in different price situations. The COL is defined for a single consumer and the form of the utility surface is not specified. It is nevertheless common practice to assume a simple form of the utility surface and to assume that a "typical" utility will represent the aggregate of consumers, for one does not expect economic rationality to hold for each individual, but it can be a reasonable hypothesis for the average behavior in a large group.

A few studies have attempted to test the difference between a COL index and fixed weight (Laspeyres) indexes. Direct comparisons with the CPI have not been made. (Phlips, 1974; Braithwait, 1975;

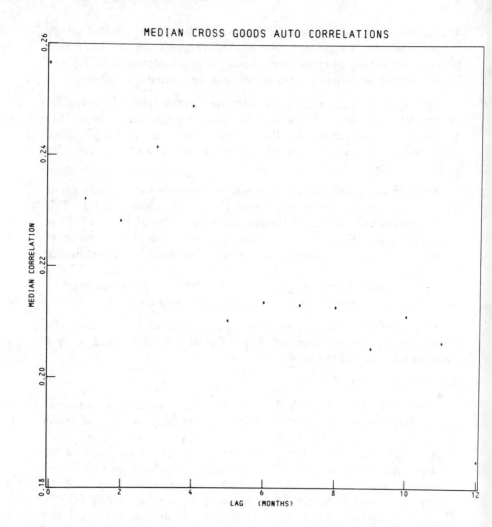

Figure 3.9
Median Cross-goods Autocorrelation

Christensen and Manser, 1974). A principal concern of these studies has been to detect the bias that has been argued to exist for a fixed weight index.[3] However, more complete arguments point out that there is not a sound theoretical basis for expecting such a bias. (Afriat, 1977).

Table 3.7 has comparisons of the following pairs of series: the Laspeyeres and True Cost of Living indexes for Belgium (Phlips,1974, Table 5.1); the Laspeyeres and Indirect Translog 1967 based indexes for meat and produce (Christensen and Manser, 1974); the Laspeyeres and Generalized Linear Expenditure System indexes from all goods, shelter, and personal services calculated by Braithwait.[4] Among the several dynamic utility functions fit by Christensen and Manser, they reported that the Indirect Translog fit best. The shelter and personal goods and services were selected from Braithwait's several subclass indexes because they had more substructure than other categories.

Table 3.7
Correlations for Laspeyeres and COL Indexes

	Commodities	Years	correlations	
			Equiweight	Biweight
Belgium	all	17	.99987	.99998
USA	meat	25	.9988	.9992
USA	produce	25	.982	.993
USA	all	17	.9990	.9986
USA	shelter	17	.9986	.9979
USA	personal services	17	.971	.978
Median			.9988	.9983

The table shows that the correlations are all quite high, compared, for instance, to those for omitted goods. The selection of countries and goods studied has been less than random, but the consistency of the results suggests that low and high estimates based on these few studies will not be incorrect to any great degree.

The formula for the effect of omission can be used for this case with $f \to 1$ and $\rho_{wy} \to \rho_{wd}$, with the estimates of Table 3.7 used for ρ_{wd}.

3. See Noe and von Furstenberg (1972), for example.
4. Braithwait did not include the indexes in his 1975 working paper; I thank him for sending them to me.

3.5 Dynamic Concepts

A cost of living index may be designed to measure dynamic effects if dynamic concepts are included in the underlying utility function. Some dynamic concepts that have been discussed are habit formation, accumulation of stocks of durable goods, and change of tastes.

There is still controversy over the desirability of including these concepts and over exactly how they should be included. Opposing viewpoints are presented by Fisher and Shell(1972) and by Phlips and Sanz-Ferrer (1975). Phlips and Sanz-Ferrer advocate a cardinal index, for which one assumes that the number (say, 20) provided by a utility formula makes sense as a "constant utility" while some parameter of the function changes. One then seeks the income required for new prices to provide the same utility. They argue, "Why not admit that utility in some base year remains the yardstick ... [and] keep everybody on the same preassigned level?" (p. 501) Fisher and Shell's theory is for an ordinal index in which one seeks the income required under new prices to remain on the same indifference surface describing current tastes that could have been reached with prior prices and income. They argue, "we have no more justification for saying that a man on the same indifference curve at two different times is equally well off at both than we do for saying that two men who happen to have the same indifference curve are equally well off if they have the same possessions." (p. 3) They further argue that the question which the true cost of living index can answer is "How much income would be required *today* to make me just indifferent between facing yesterday's budget constraint and facing a budget constraint defined by today's prices and the income [now available]?" (p. 4) They note, "it is a question posed entirely in terms of today's tastes...." (p. 4) Fisher and Shell concentrate conceptually on taste changes from external influences such as information from neighbors, advertising, or demonstrations. Phlips and Sanz-Ferrer concentrate on the impact of past decisions, pointing out that external information may lead to the formation of habits or inventories.

Phlips and Sanz-Ferrer made estimates of dynamic COL indexes based on both these viewpoints. They used a modified form of the common Stone-Geary utility function, which has as a parameter a "minimum" or "necessary" quantity. They modify the static function by allowing the "minimum" quantity to reflect habit formation (in which more of a good comes to be required for the same utility) or inventory satiation (in which less of a good comes to be required for the same utility). Phlips and Sanz-Ferrer point out that, in selecting a dynamic index, both short-run and long-run parameters can be used. They calculated both, and stated that they considered the long-run index uninteresting because equilibrium would not be reached in each successive period. It would seem that the most appropriate parameters would be those matched to the interval for which prices were being assembled, whether a month, a quarter, or a year. Presumably, each of these would lie between the short-run index and the long-run index. Phlips and Sanz-Ferrer give Laspeyeres, cardinal, and ordinal indexes for the short-run and Laspeyeres and cardinal indexes for the long-run. The short-run cardinal index shows a larger mean price change than do the others, due to a predominance of habit formation among the goods, and the concomitant need for more of the goods for the same utility. Furthermore, as Table 3.8 shows, the cardinal index is distinctly less correlated with either the Laspeyeres or ordinal index than are the Laspeyeres and ordinal indexes. The correlation between the long-run Laspeyeres and cardinal indexes is much larger.

Table 3.8
Correlations for Dynamic Concepts

	Correlations	
	Equiweight	Biweight
Short-run		
Laspeyeres-cardinal	.987	.964
Laspeyeres-ordinal	.996	.992
cardinal-ordinal	.989	.978
Long-run		
Laspeyeres-cardinal	.997	.9993

The three correlations from Table 3.8 which compare a Laspeyeres index with another index were used in the formula for omission with $f=1$.

3.6 Specification and Quality

A recent review of price index accuracy by Triplett (1977) is particularly useful for its discussion of quality changes. Triplett remarks that many economists have considered quality change to be the major problem for price indexes. In this discussion, "quality" does not refer to a subjective phenomenon, but rather to unmeasured attributes. For instance, if a price is quoted per candy bar, and the weight changes from 2.0 ounces to 1.8 ounces, a change in quality has taken place. Or if the price is quoted per ounce of candy and if the percent of chocolate changes from 35 percent to 25 percent, a change in quality has taken place.

Quality is therefore a specific instance of the more general problem of specification of the goods to price. Most of the available results on the effect of specification are given for quality changes.

Currently the Bureau of Labor Statistics uses the following procedure to adjust for some changes in quality. If price information is available for the change — which is the case only for automobiles in the CPI — the price change is taken net of the value of the quality changes. In other cases, the commodity specialist (of whom there are about forty for the CPI, and a like number for the PPI) judges whether the quality change is *major* or *minor*. If the change is judged to be minor, then it is assumed that the price of the quality change was zero, and the observed price change is entered without adjustment. If the quality change is judged to be major, then the good is "linked in." That is, it is assumed that the price change of that good for that month is the same as that for all other goods of its kind that are included in the index that month. This assumes that the price of the quality change was the difference between the actual price change for the linked good and the average price change for other goods of its kind. Ideally, we would like to know the difference between *this* quality procedure and any other quality procedure.

The leading alternative is called the "hedonic," or "attribute," method. First more data are gathered about the attributes of the goods surveyed, for example, the volume of a refrigerator, the horsepower of its motor, and whether it has an icemaker. Then a regression, usually cross sectional, is used to impute prices to the attributes. There are a number of open questions about exactly how this should be done, such as how frequently to update the regression and how to use data from more than one year. The price change of a good can then be taken net of the value of quality changes.

In the last twenty years a few dozen studies have used the attribute method to assess quality changes in particular goods. Unfortunately, most of the studies cover only a few years, and many have several differences other than quality from any government series. Thus many of the studies are not useful for judging how the CPI would change if a different quality adjustment process were used.

Another quality adjustment process is the "vintage" method, which involves collecting data on used goods. A pure rate of depreciation is established, and remaining price differences are attributed to quality differences. The method can be applied only retroactively, which would preclude its use in the CPI under current guidelines, and it can be applied only where there are major markets for the used goods. In practice, it has been limited in its application to automobiles and trucks. For these reasons, this paper has not included studies using the vintage method.

Table 3.9 summarizes the results from studies with the longest series and the most comparable to government series. The studies are presented in order of decreasing number of years of prices adjusted. All the studies reported results on an annual basis, and the data for each can be found either in Triplett (1977) or Triplett(1971).

Two indexes for cars from the Ohta and Griliches (1976) study of automobile prices show the importance of details of the attribute method. The two were constructed from the same data, but one included dummy variables for the make of car in the attribute regression, and one did not. The second and third rows of the table show the correlation of these two indexes with the CPI automobile component. As can be seen, the correlations estimated are quite different. The correlation of the two indexes themselves is .91 (.92 biweighted). There are coverage differences (makes of cars) for the Ohta and Griliches autos and used autos indexes as well as quality differences from the CPI. Therefore, this study has used only the higher of the two correlation estimates for autos.

The correlation shown in the last row of the table is that between columns 1 and 6 of Table 2-4 in Triplett (1977). It is a comparison with a list price index and not a government index, but it does differ only in quality from the index used.

The refrigerators, suits, and tractors studies differed only in quality from the WPI. Thus there are no studies that differ only in quality from a subindex of the CPI.

It is also worth noting, as an example of specification difference, that Triplett (1977) presents (in column 4 of Table 2-4) a series that appears to differ from his corrected CPI (column 3 of Table 2-4) only by treatment of dealer concessions. Yet the correlation is only .27 (.28 biweighted). This study has not included this low correlation among those to estimate specification differences. The annual measurement error is thus calculated with the biweighted correlations shown in Table 3.9, excepting the third line of the table.

Table 3.9
Quality Adjustment Studies

Subject	Years	Correlations		Comparison	Authors
		Equiweight	Biweight		
Refrigerators	12	.85	.91	WPI	Triplett and McDonald (1975)
Autos (make)	11	.74	.71	CPI	Ohta and Griliches (1976)
Autos (no make)	11	(.58)	(.52)	CPI	"
Used autos	10	.45	.47	CPI	"
Tractors	10	.78	.73	WPI	Fettig (1963)
Men's suits	8	.93	.95	WPI	Gavett (1967)
Autos	7	.85	.86	list price	Griliches (1961)

While there are no published data for quality studies on a monthly or quarterly basis, McDonald has most graciously provided monthly series that formed the basis of Table 5 in Triplett and McDonald (1975). Figure 3.10 is a plot of the quality-adjusted refrigerator-freezer component of the WPI against the unadjusted component. The adjusted component shown is the one based on correction of 1960-1965 data with attribute values from a regression of 1963-1965 data, and correction of 1966-1972 data with attribute values from a regression of 1969-1972 data (column C of their Table 5). Note that both of these include retrospective adjustments. The line on the figure is the line of equality. The figure shows a backbone of equality within rounding factors, and twenty-eight months with differences. In this situation, a biweight correlation is misleading because the "outliers" *are* the data. To check the equiweight correlation coefficient of .87, this study used the following model.

The adjustment is either zero with some probability denoted α, or it is drawn from a population of mean zero and variance σ^2. Then the correlation between the adjusted series and the unadjusted series will be given by $1/(1 + \alpha\sigma^2/V_X)$ where V_X is the variance of the original series. This shows that as α goes to zero, σ goes to zero, or V_X goes to infinity, while the others remain constant, the correlation will go to one. The probability of a zero correction is estimated from the data as $\alpha = .79$. When equiweight estimates of σ^2 and V_X are used, we recover the equiweight correlation estimate. The variance of the nonzero corrections is estimated as $\sigma^2 = 1.7 \ x \ 10^{-4}$ by the biweight variance of the nonzero changes, and the variance of the original series is estimated as $V_x = 1.2 \ x \ 10^{-6}$ from the biweight variance of the unadjusted series. A robust estimate of the correlation is then suggested to be $(1/(1 + \alpha\sigma^2/V_x))^{\frac{1}{2}} = .54$. The difference from the ordinary correlation is primarily in the treatment of the two points that had large decreases and no quality changes. These two points greatly influence the estimate of V_X. Since there were only two such points, it was quite likely that there would not also be a quality correction at the same time. For this reason, I find the robust estimate more convincing than the equiweight estimate. The corresponding equiweight and robust correlations for the same series taken on a quarterly basis are .84 and .77.

Another aspect of the data is shown in Figure 3.11, which is a scatter plot of the autocorrelation of the unadjusted series. It shows that zero price change is a very common occurrence in the data, so that the points are concentrated along the two axes. The appearance of the figure is probably tied to the fact that the corrections are being made to

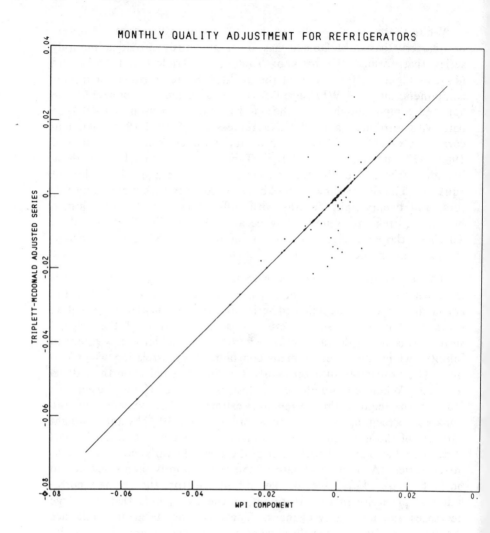

MONTHLY QUALITY ADJUSTMENT FOR REFRIGERATORS

Figure 3.10
Monthly Quality Adjustment for Refrigerators

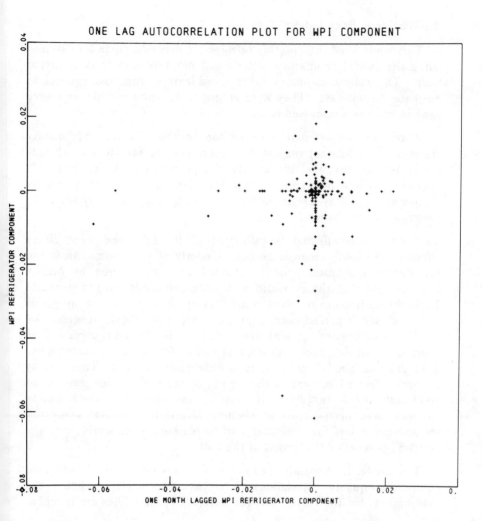

Figure 3.11
One-lag Autocorrelation Plot for WPI Component

the Wholesale Price Index.

This study used the monthly refrigerator data as a guide for extrapolating the annual results to quarterly and monthly periods as discussed later. The robust estimates differ considerably from the equiweight estimates in this case. They were judged to be more reliable, and were used in estimates discussed later.

It remains to estimate the fraction of the CPI that has quality changes of the amount suggested by these few studies. It is worth noting in this context that the quality change problem shades into style changes and into new goods. Here the many other studies of quality change also can play a legitimate role in suggesting that many goods do undergo quality changes.

The amount affected is estimated as if each good were either affected by quality changes or not. Underlying this estimation is the supposition that each good is affected to some degree by quality changes, but that the corrections to different goods are independent. Then the estimation involves simply trying to guess how many goods will be closer to perfect correlation than to the correlation suggested by the four studies cited. A high amount of goods affected is suggested by supposing that only fuel, utilities, and half of food at home (being quite homogeneous goods) are subject to little quality change. Then quality changes affect 83 percent of the weight of the CPI. A low amount of goods affected is suggested by detailing the goods for which quality changes have been observed: shelter, furnishings, women's apparel, transportation less fuel, medical, and recreation. Then quality changes affect 52 percent of the weight of the CPI.

The model in Appendix Section A.4 relates estimates of individual component quality correlations to an overall correlation under the assumption that the corrections for different commodities are independent.

3.7 Sampling

The design of the price sample collected allows the BLS to estimate the error due to sampling. The price sample replicates items and outlets and pairs sampled cities (those with populations under 3 million).

Table 3.10 shows the published figures in the second column. These are stated as the standard deviation of the sampling error in units of percent change. In the third column, these numbers have been divided by the standard deviation of the price changes for the appropriate time period. The final column is used with equation 9-43 of Johnston (1972) to calculate the bias factor for this effect, assuming for this effect that the error is independent of the deflator and the nominal price.

Table 3.10
Magnitude of Sampling Errors

	Standard Deviation Percent Change	Standard Deviation Fraction of S.D.(CPI)
Monthly	.04	.13
Quarterly	.05	.065
Annually	.10	.034

4. Differences Not Quantified

Before comparing the quantified effects, let us briefly review some other differences that may be important in econometric analyses.

First, any effect that gives an unknown bias also contributes to the variance of errors unless it is known that the bias is always constant. As mentioned before, new goods are a possible source of bias.

Second, there are other dimensions to "price" than just the monetary component. Another major component is time to acquire, and a third is availability. These other dimensions are most likely to change during times of war and/or price controls, but they have also affected the price of gasoline in the last ten years. Some analysts, including Fama (1975), have omitted such years from their studies rather than accept the available measures of monetary price change, so this may be a severe effect.

Other differences may be associated with retail rebates (such as food store coupons) and strongly seasonal goods.

5. Correction for Bias

The calculation presented here allows a first order correction for the expected bias. For the criterion model, the appropriate correction is

$$\overset{\approx}{b} = \frac{\hat{b}}{1 + \phi}$$

since

$$plim\,(\overset{*}{b}) = \frac{plim\,(\hat{b})}{1 + \phi} = b$$

and is thus asymptotically unbiased. In practical models with many variables, this remains a first order correction whose accuracy depends on the correlations between the deflated variable and other exogenous variables.

Suppose that only the first variable, x_1, is deflated, and that only it is subject to error. Then if it is independent of the other exogenous variables, the corrections given here can be applied to the first coefficient. Appendix Section A.1 gives a generic formula for the asymptotic bias in an OLS equation as

$$plim\,(\hat{\beta}) - \beta = -plim\,(\frac{1}{n}X'X)^{-1}\,plim\,(\frac{1}{n}X'V)\beta$$

where $\hat{\beta}$ is the vector of estimates of β, X is the matrix of observations, and V is the matrix of errors. Then $X'X$ decomposes into $x'_1 x_1$ and an orthogonal part $X_-'X_-$:

$$X'X = \begin{bmatrix} x_1 x_1 & 0 \\ 0 & X_-'X_- \end{bmatrix}$$

and its inverse is

$$(X'X)^{-1} = \begin{bmatrix} (x_1 x_1)^{-1} & 0 \\ 0 & (X_-'X_-)^{-1} \end{bmatrix}$$

Thus the first coefficient is isolated from the rest.

If those assumptions are not useful, we need a correction to each coefficient whose corresponding variable is correlated with the deflator. In particular, we can expect that when two or more variables are measured in nominal terms, each will be correlated with the deflator. Then the bias in each such estimated coefficient depends on each other such coefficient, and if we have

$$plim\,(\hat{\beta}) = \left[1 + \Phi\right]\beta$$

where 1 is an identity matrix, we can use

$$\overset{*}{\beta} = \left[1 + \Phi\right]\hat{\beta}$$

as an asymptotically unbiased estimator. Each element of Φ can be taken from results presented here.

A temptation might be to enter the deflator separately from nominal quantities to deflate. Supposing that the nominal quantities were measured without error, we might then expect their coefficients to be unbiased, while the bias was concentrated in the coefficient of the deflator. However, this prospect is illusory, since correlation between the deflator and the nominal variables results in the same bias to the coefficients of the nominal variables.

The bias can be corrected exactly only if the variance and correlations of the error are known exactly. This information is not available, so the uncertainty in the bias correction will become another source of uncertainty in the coefficient. A goal of this paper has been to suggest a plausible range of uncertainty in the bias correction so that this uncertainty in the coefficient can be combined with other known uncertainties.

6. Comparison of Effects

The quantitative goals of this paper are to give approximate magnitudes to the errors incurred by using the CPI as a deflator in econometric work. If no correction is made for the errors discussed, the first-order effect is a bias in the regression coefficient. The biases could be discussed and compared using the medians of the various sets of correlations that have been discussed. However, if the bias is corrected for, there remains the uncertainty in the estimates presented here. To present an estimate of the remaining variability requires some characterization of the distributions of the sets of correlations and amounts estimated. To do this, I constructed a simulation of the errors. The simulation uses each set of correlation estimates as a point distribution, each estimate being given equal weight. One hundred simulation trials are used, with each uncertain factor independently chosen at random from the observed or assumed distribution. The result is 100 estimates of the error from each cause, judged to be equally likely as estimates of the error from that cause. After calculating the simulated distribution of errors from each cause, I combined the errors as explained later, giving 100 estimates of the overall effect that were judged equally likely. These simulated distributions should give some idea of the uncertainty of our knowledge of the errors.

6.1 Extrapolation

For each error source we have estimated an annual correlation. For four error sources (shown at the left of Table 3.11), we have both annual and quarterly correlation estimates. For three, we have both quarterly and monthly estimates. We need to estimate four more quarterly correlations and five more monthly correlations. To do so, we will assume some simple relation between correlation and time period, calibrate the relation on the directly estimated correlations, and extrapolate using the relation to estimate the remaining correlations.

Three simple relations between correlation and time period were considered: (1)Correlation as a linear function of time period. A problem here is that differences between high correlations (say, over .99) are not expected to be comparable to differences between moderate correlations. The Fisher Z-transform of correlations as a linear function of time period. This solves the first objection. However, a negative correlation might be extrapolated from a small positive one. The logarithm of correlation as a linear function of time period. This assumption guarantees that an extrapolation from a near-zero correlation will remain positive and near zero. The third method was used.

Table 3.11 shows the available data for calibrating the assumed logarithmic relation. The slopes are represented as a power, for instance, .51 is the 5.3 power of .88. The power for city size is very large compared to the rest and is not used for extrapolation. The powers for refrigerator quality are the smallest for both annual to quarterly and for quarterly to monthly; they were used to extrapolate the annual quality correlations to quarterly and monthly values. The set of the six smallest powers was used to extrapolate correlations for dynamic effects, substitution effects, and omitted consumers. That is, the set was used as a point distribution in the simulation for these errors.

Table 3.11
Correlations Used for Extrapolation

Error Source	Correlations		Power	Correlations		Power
	A	Q		Q	M	
Commodity omis.	.88	.51	5.3	.51	.20	2.4
Refrigerator qual.	.88	.77	2.0	.77	.54	2.4
Sampling error	.9994	.9984	2.7	.9984	.9915	5.3
City size	.989	.58	49			

6.2 Individual Effects

For this comparison, the procedures assumed are those currently in use. That is, if the current procedures were unchanged for ten years, a criterion regression using ten years' data could be done in 1988 with biases as shown in the Figures 3.12 to 3.15. This is appropriate because the purpose of comparing individual effects is to guide further research into their magnitudes and to suggest priorities for the change of current procedures. The correlations used were the biweight correlations.

Figures 3.12 through 3.16 are "box plots" showing the results of the error simulation. The "boxes" consist of five parts, the upper and lower whiskers, the upper and lower edges of the boxes, and the line in the middle of the box. The upper and lower whiskers mark the upper and lower extremes taken by a set of data; the upper and lower edges mark the upper and lower quartiles, and the line in the middle marks the median. Each box in Figure 3.12 and the following figures represents distributions of 100 points resulting from 100 simulation runs. Note, however, that the scales of Figures 3.12 through 3.15 are not comparable. These figures are designed for the comparison of the magnitudes from various effects, not the comparison by time period. Figure 3.16 gives the comparison by time period.

Figure 3.12 compares the annual effects by type of error. It indicates that the worst problems among those quantified are quality adjustment and goods omission. Their median errors are close, but goods omission could be much worse. The third problem is dynamic definition. Its median is half as bad as the first two, but it could be as bad. No other source of error is likely to cause as much bias as 1 percent. In particular, sampling is a very small contributor. If this is true for other uses of the CPI as well, it might be reasonable to reduce the size of the sample and use the resources to improve the quality adjustment processes and the goods coverage. The effect for time period mismatches is small but positive, while all others are negative. Correlations between the error and the true deflator are quite important for the time period mismatch effect, as it is a sum of oppositely directed effects. Figure 3.13 plots the same information as the logarithm (base 10) of the absolute value of the fractional error. This allows us to see the relative uncertainties for the smaller factors such as omitted consumers. The relative uncertainties are largest for substitution effects and dynamic effects, and smallest for sampling.

Figure 3.14 shows the comparison of effects for quarterly time periods. Both quality and dynamic effects are being extrapolated, and their relationship must remain fixed. The omitted consumers have become more important, exceeding quality and omitted goods. Each of the major effects is estimated to become larger in magnitude. This is again partly a result of the extrapolations.

Figure 3.15 shows the individual effects for monthly periods. Quality is clearly the worst problem for monthly measurement, with omitted goods and consumers following.

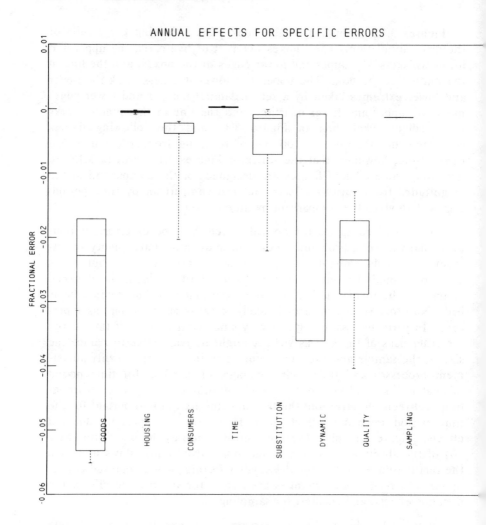

Figure 3.12
Annual Effects for Specific Errors, Absolute Scale

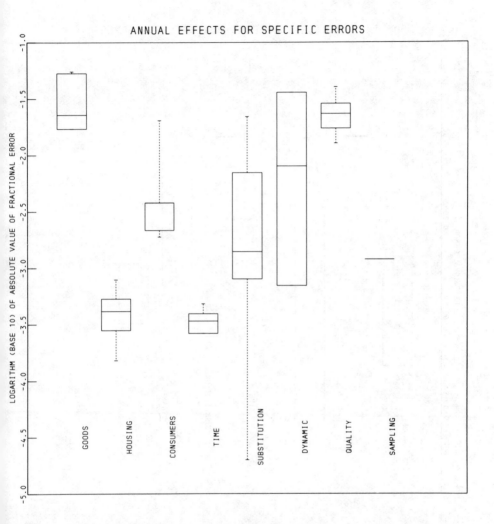

Figure 3.13
Annual Effects for Specific Errors, Logarithmic Scale

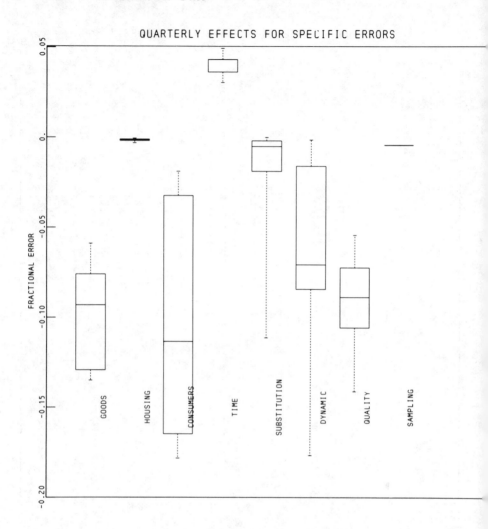

Figure 3.14
Quarterly Effects for Specific Errors

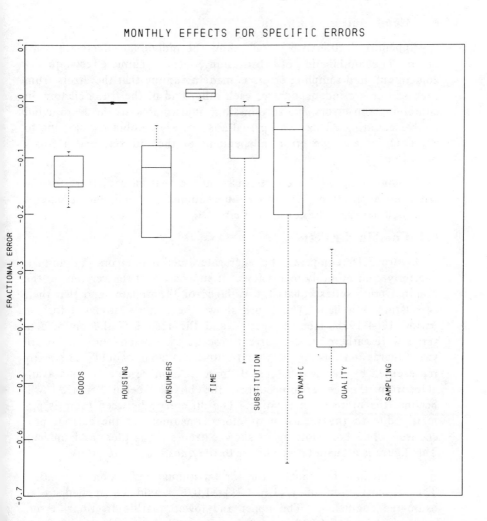

Figure 3.15
Monthly Effects for Specific Errors

6.3 Combination of Effects

Appendix Section A.6 details how the individual effects are combined. The combination of substitution effects, dynamic effects, quality adjustment, and sampling errors is made assuming that the errors from each source are independent of each other and of the true deflator. In combining the errors due to omission, adjustments are made to avoid double counting. These two partial answers are combined according to a model for a single error independent of the indexes, and a single omission.

In combining all the effects, it is judged that all are errors for the criterion application. In other applications, not all the problems identified here may be considered errors.

6.4 Combined Effects

Figure 3.16 compares the aggregate fractional errors for annual, quarterly, and monthly regressions. It supposes that the variance of the nominal price series equals the variance of the deflator and that their correlation is a half. The figure shows the results estimated for the period 1964-1978, labeled "past," and the results if the entire data series were gathered under current procedures, labeled "future." A ten year regression using data currently available would be nearly represented by the figures labeled "past." As more data become available from the newer procedures, the boxes labeled "future" will become the more representative. The difference between them is primarily due to the inclusion of more consumers in the current procedures. The box plots again show extremes, quartiles, and median. This figure is a quantitative answer to the question of the title.

The median fractional error for an annual regression is $-.071$. Thus a correction of $1/(1 - .071) = 1.076$ would be applied to an estimated coefficient. The upper and lower quartile fractional errors give corrections of 1.094 and 1.055, so that the corrected estimate could be off by 2 percent on either side due to uncertainties in the correction process. The correction for a quarterly regression would be a factor of $1/(1 - .40) = 1.67$, with quartile correction factors of $1.85 = 1/(1 - .46)$ and $1.35 = 1/(1 - .26)$. The correction for a monthly regression would be a factor of $1/(1. - 66) = 2.9$, with quartile correction factors of $3.7 = 1/(1 - .73)$ and $2.4 = 1/(1 - .58)$. The uncertainty here is exacerbated by the necessity to extrapolate what are certainly large effects, but which can be only guessed at now.

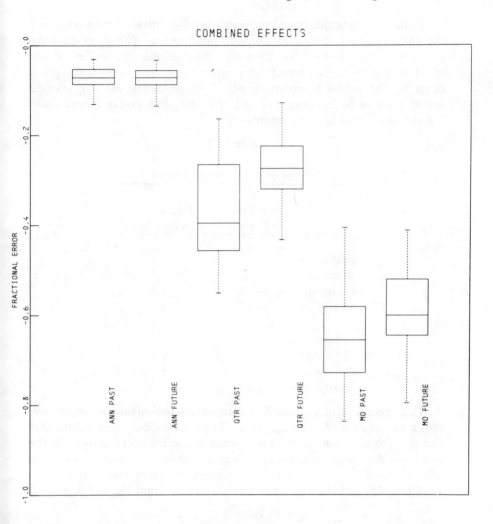

Figure 3.16
Combined Effects

Table 3.12 lists the fractional errors for the criterion regression and the corresponding equivalent signal-to-noise ratios. The signal-to-noise ratios are less than 1 for monthly observations. In effect, single monthly observations contain little information; the importance given them by the media is unwarranted. A three-month moving average would begin to be interesting in and of itself, and a twelve month moving average would be quite interesting.

Table 3.12

Effects of Uncorrected Errors

	Fractional Error	Equivalent Signal-to-Noise
Past		
Monthly	−.65	0.5
Quarterly	−.40	1.5
Yearly	−.07	13
Future		
Monthly	−.60	0.7
Quarterly	−.26	3
Yearly	−.07	13

The preceding discussion has focused on the effects when the criterion values of $\tau = 1$ and $\rho_{pw} = \frac{1}{2}$. Table 3.1 set out some values of τ and ρ_{pw} from a few specific price series. The fractional errors for the problems discussed with those values are shown in Table 3.13. The table shows the fractional errors for regressions using data of the period 1964 to 1978, and shows only the median result from the simulation.

Table 3.13
Effects for Specific Price Series

	Time Period		
	Year	Quarter	Month
Jurisdiction A	−.007	−.009	−.008
All intrastate LD	−.096	−.31	−.13
Major commodities	−.22	−.40	−.41

Notice first that in jurisdiction A, the variance of the long distance price changes was sufficiently large that none of the corrections exceeds 1 percent. The table also shows that the larger errors for quarterly and monthly periods in the criterion regression tend to be offset by larger relative variances for their price series. Results such as these should be used in deciding on the period to use for a specific regression. The second row of the table shows that the quarterly period is not necessarily to be preferred to the monthly, for instance.

7. Summary

The errors from deflator measurement error need to be considered in econometric work. In cases for which the nominal variable has a large variance compared to the deflator, the effects of deflator error will not be important. If the nominal price variance is comparable to or smaller than the deflator variance, a first order correction for bias can be made. The corrections suggested are substantial for quarterly and monthly regressions. There remains a small uncertainty for annual regressions, a moderate uncertainty for quarterly regressions, and a large uncertainty for monthly regressions if each satisfies the criterion assumptions.

This paper shows the need for research on the quarterly and monthly effects for quality, dynamic effects, and consumer omission. If the primary concern is to improve quarterly data, then omission of goods is quite as important an error as quality correction.

Appendix A

A.1 A General Formulation and Reduction

This section introduces a notation for discussing errors in variables, which is that of Johnston (1972). It then reduces the generality to that of the criterion regression. Each later section in the appendix starts from the reduced form to model the effects of a specific error.

The observed data matrix of explanatory variables for an OLS regression is

$$\mathbf{X} = \tilde{\mathbf{X}} + \mathbf{V}$$

where $\tilde{\mathbf{X}}$ denotes the matrix of true values and $\mathbf{V}$ is a matrix of measurement errors. The observed values of $\mathbf{q}$ are given by

$$\mathbf{q} = \tilde{\mathbf{X}}\beta + \mathbf{u}$$
$$= \mathbf{X}\beta + (\mathbf{u} - \mathbf{V}\beta)$$

where β is a vector of coefficients. Assuming $\mathbf{X}'\mathbf{X}$ is invertible, the OLS estimate of β is

$$\hat{\beta} = (X'X)^{-1}X'q$$
$$= \beta + (X'X)^{-1}(X'u - X'V\beta)$$

and

$$plim\,(\hat{\beta}) = \beta + plim\,(\frac{1}{n}X'X)^{-1}[plim\,(\frac{1}{n}X'u) - plim\,(\frac{1}{n}X'V)\beta]$$

It is reasonable to suppose that $plim\,(\frac{1}{n}X'u) = 0$, which is a statement that real and measured variations in q not due to X are uncorrelated with either the true values $\tilde{X}$ or its measurement errors V. This leaves

$$plim\,(\hat{\beta}) = \beta - plim\,(\frac{1}{n}X'X)^{-1}plim\,(\frac{1}{n}X'V)\beta$$

Now the criterion regression has only a constant term and a single exogenous variable. Thus $\tilde{X}$ and X are of the form

$$\tilde{X} = (1,\tilde{x})$$
$$X = (1,x)$$

where 1 is a column vector of ones, and $\tilde{x}$ and x are column vectors of true and observed values. Thus

$$V = (0,x-\tilde{x}) \equiv (0,v)$$

and

$$plim\,(\frac{1}{n}X'V) = \begin{bmatrix} 0 & plim\,(\frac{1}{n}\sum_{i=1}^{n}(x_i - \tilde{x}_i)) \\ 0 & plim\,(\frac{1}{n}\sum_{i=1}^{n}x_i v_i) \end{bmatrix}$$

$$\equiv \begin{bmatrix} 0 & E(X-\tilde{X}) \\ 0 & E(XV) \end{bmatrix}$$

This work assumes that x is an unbiased measure of $\tilde{x}$, so

$$E(X-\tilde{X}) = 0$$

Then there is no error in the constant term of the regression, and asymptotic fractional error in the slope term is

$$\phi \equiv \frac{plim\,(\hat{b}) - b}{b} = -\frac{E(XV)}{E(XX)}$$

Note that if V is independent of $\tilde{X}$, then $\phi < 0$, which implies that the estimated coefficient, $\hat{b}$, is asymptotically biased toward zero. The observed deflator is always written as w, and

$$E(XX) = E((p-w)(p-w)) = \sigma_p^2 - 2\sigma_p\sigma_w\rho_{pw} + \sigma_w^2$$
$$= (\tau^2 - 2\tau\rho_{pw} + 1)\sigma_w^2$$

where $\tau = \sigma_p/\sigma_w$. Thus

$$\phi = -\frac{E(XV)/\sigma_w^2}{\tau^2 - 2\tau\rho_{pw} + 1}.$$

This is the reduced form that will be used in other sections.

A.2 Effect of Omission

The formula developed in this section is used for calculating most of the effects. The true deflator is

$$d = (1-f)w + fy$$

while the measured deflator is w. We have

$$\tilde{X} = p - d$$
$$X = p - w$$
$$V = X - \tilde{X} = (p-w) - (p-d) = d - w$$
$$= f(y-w).$$

and

$$E(XV) = E[(p-w)f(y-w)]$$
$$= f[\sigma_p\sigma_y\rho_{py} - \sigma_p\sigma_w\rho_{pw} - \sigma_w\sigma_y\rho_{wy} + \sigma_w^2]$$

This depends on the observed σ_p, σ_w, f, and ρ_{px}, and also on σ_y, ρ_{xy}, and ρ_{py}. The text uses several methods for indirectly estimating ρ_{wy}, and we regard it as observed. We must make assumptions to give estimates for σ_y and ρ_{py}. It is quite reasonable to assume $\sigma_y = \sigma_w$. For the five major commodity groups described in Section 3.1, the standard deviations of monthly price changes have been 6.04, 5.95, 5.63, 5.59, and 6.17 percent per year. Then

$$\phi = -f\frac{\tau(\rho_{py} - \rho_{pw}) + (1 - \rho_{wy})}{\tau^2 - 2\tau\rho_{pw} + 1}$$

The correlation between the nominal price changes p_t and the changes in the omitted part of the deflator y_t is not known. A confession of ignorance may be less damaging than a poor assumption here. For the purposes of the criterion, then, this study has taken $\rho_{py} = \rho_{pw}$. Nor is it clear how to get a sense of how wrong this may be in order to simulate the error. For this reason, among others, the variability of the fractional errors presented here is a cautious estimate.

The equation used to calculate the effect of an omission is thus

$$\phi = -\frac{f(1 - \rho_{wy})}{\tau^2 - 2\tau\rho_{pw} + 1}.$$

A.3 Housing Model

We assume that the true and measured deflators are

$$d = (1 - f - g)x + gz + fy$$
$$w = (1 - f - g)x + gz + fz$$

where y represents a lower-price housing index and z represents a higher-price housing index. The model assumptions are

$$\rho_{xy} = \rho_{xz}$$
$$\rho_{py} = \rho_{pz}$$
$$\sigma_y = \sigma_z$$

Then

$$V = (p - w) - (p - d)$$
$$= f(y - z).$$

and

$$\begin{aligned}
E(XV) &= fE[(p - w)(y - z)] \\
&= -fE(w(y - z)) \\
&= -f[(1 - f - g)(\rho_{xy} - \rho_{xz}) + (g + f)(\rho_{yz} - 1)]\sigma_z^2 \\
&= f(f + g)(1 - \rho_{yz})\sigma_z^2
\end{aligned}$$

And approximating $\sigma_z^2/\sigma_w^2 \approx 1$,

$$\phi = -\frac{f(f + g)(1 - \rho_{yz})}{\tau^2 - 2\tau\rho_{pw} + 1}$$

On the assumption that the substitute series has similar correlation to the rest of the index, the effect is less severe than a simple omission.

A.4 Quality Model

The basic formula is the formula for omission with $f = 1$ (and hence $y \to d$ and $\rho_{yw} \to \rho_{dw}$), but we estimate ρ_{dw} from the following model.

The text gives estimates for the quality errors of a few specific goods. Several hundred such goods are included in the CPI. If each is independent, then the net effect may be negligible by cancellation of errors.

Suppose that the true index for each good included is d_i. The measurement without quality accounting is

$$x_i = d_i + \epsilon_i \quad i = 1,...,fI$$
$$= d_i \quad i = fI1,...,I$$

We assume the measurement errors ϵ_i are independent of each other and of the x_i. For instance, the quality measurement errors of coats are independent of the quality measurement errors for peanut butter, and of the price changes for coats. Denote the variance of d_i by σ_i^2 and of ϵ_i by τ_i^2. The aggregate price change is

$$d = \sum_{i=1}^{I} \alpha_i d_i$$

while that estimated is

$$w = \sum_{i=1}^{I} \alpha_i x_i$$

Then the variance of d is

$$V_d = \sum_{i=1}^{I} \alpha_i^2 \sigma_i^2 + \sum_{i \neq j} \alpha_i \alpha_j \sigma_i \sigma_j \rho_{ij}$$

The second term has many more parameters than we can estimate. We approximate it as

$$\sum_{i \neq j} \alpha_i \alpha_j \sigma_i \sigma_j \rho_{ij} = k \sum_{i=1}^{I} \alpha_i^2 \sigma_i^2$$

Notice that if $\alpha_i = 1/I$, $\sigma_i = \sigma$, and $\rho_{ij} = \rho$, then $k = I\rho$, which can be quite large.

We can examine the variance of w, which is

$$V_w = V_d + \sum_{i=1}^{fI} \alpha_i^2 \tau_i^2$$

and also the sum of variances of individual series

$$\sum_{i=1}^{I} \alpha_i^2 V_{x_i} = \sum_{i=1}^{I} \alpha_i^2 \sigma_i^2 + \sum_{i=1}^{fI} \alpha_i^2 \tau_i^2$$

The results for eighteen second-level commodities of the CPI are

	$\sum_{i=1}^{18} \alpha_i^2 V_{x_i}$	V_w
Monthly	$4.1 \cdot 10^{-6}$	$8.3 \cdot 10^{-6}$

$$\begin{array}{lll} \text{Quarterly} & 2.0 \cdot 10^{-5} & 5.8 \cdot 10^{-5} \\ \text{Annual} & 1.2 \cdot 10^{-4} & 7.6 \cdot 10^{-4} \end{array}$$

Now we have estimated a few of

$$\rho^2_{x_i d_i} = \frac{\sigma_i^2}{\sigma_i^2 + \tau_i^2} = \frac{1}{1 + \tau_i^2/\sigma_i^2}$$

We assume that the τ_i^2/σ_i^2 so estimated represents the ratio $\sum_{i=1}^{I}\alpha_i^2\tau_i^2 / \sum_{i=1}^{I}\alpha_i^2\sigma_i^2$, although clearly our knowledge falls short of that desired. That is (dropping the specializing subscripts on the ρ),

$$\frac{\displaystyle\sum_{i=1}^{I}\alpha_i^2\tau_i^2}{\displaystyle\sum_{i=1}^{I}\alpha_i^2} = \rho^{-2} - 1$$

We also assume

$$\sum_{i=1}^{fI}\alpha_i^2\tau_i^2 = f \sum_{i=1}^{I}\alpha_i^2\tau_i^2$$

which seems reasonable for the several hundred goods involved. Then

$$\sum_{i=1}^{I}\alpha_i^2 V_{x_i} = \sum_{i=1}^{I}\alpha_i^2\sigma_i^2 + \sum_{i=1}^{fI}\alpha_i^2\tau_i^2$$
$$= \sum_{i=1}^{I}\alpha_i^2\sigma_i^2(1 + f\,(\rho^{-2} - 1))$$

while

$$V_w = (k + 1) \sum_{i=1}^{I}\alpha_i^2\sigma_i^2 + f \sum_{i=1}^{I}\alpha_i^2\tau_i^2$$
$$= (k + 1 + f(\rho^{-2} - 1)) \sum_{i=1}^{I}\alpha_i^2\sigma_i^2$$

Therefore

$$\frac{k + 1 + f(\rho^{-2} - 1)}{1 + f(\rho^{-2} - 1)} = \frac{V_w}{\displaystyle\sum_{i=1}^{I}\alpha_i^2 V_{x_i}}$$

can be solved for k. Finally, the quantity that we need is ρ_{dw}, calculated by

$$\rho_{dw} = \frac{V_d}{V_w}$$

$$= \frac{k+1}{k+1+f(\rho^{-2}-1)}$$

This formula calls for an estimate of a mean correlation, ρ. In the simulation described in Section 6, a distribution for this mean was provided by scaling each of the six correlations used toward the median by the square root of six. This accounts for the greater certainty that we have in a mean than we have in any one estimate.

A.5 Time Period Mismatch

The available facts allow a fairly detailed calculation for time period mismatches. The many possible parameters could lead to a very complicated model, but the model used here suggests that the effect is not so large as to justify more detail.

We first make a preliminary calculation that is a basis for six submodels. One submodel is necessary for each of monthly, quarterly, and annual time periods. In addition, one submodel is required for the period before 1968 when there were three staggered subperiods of measurement, and another submodel is required for the period after 1968 when there are but two staggered subperiods.

Denote the true deflator changes by

$$d_t = x_t + y_t$$

where x_t represents all measurements made monthly, and y_t represents the changes for the remainder if they were measured monthly. But

$$w_t = x_t + z_t$$

is used instead, where z_t is the actual measurement for nonmonthly goods and places. The weighting of these will be introduced by the structure assigned to the x, y, and z. We also denote

$$z_t = y_t + \psi_t$$

Since we suppose that w_t is an unbiased estimator of d_t, we have $E(\psi) = 0$. Then suppressing the t subscripts, we have

$$V = d - w$$
$$= y - z$$
$$= -\psi$$

and

$$E(XV) = E(-wV)$$
$$= E(w\psi)$$
$$= E((d + \psi)\psi)$$
$$= E(d\psi) + E(\psi^2)$$

But we can now calculate

$$\sigma_w^2 = \sigma_d^2 + 2E(d\psi) + E(\psi^2)$$

Then

$$\phi = \frac{1}{\tau^2 - 2\tau\rho_{pw} + 1} \frac{E(d\psi) + E(\psi^2)}{\sigma_d^2 + 2E(d\psi) + E(\psi^2)}$$

This completes the preliminary calculation. We now give one example of a time period submodel in detail.

We use the simple model of correlations for different cities and time periods discussed in Section 3.3. We introduce the variables m_{ik} and n_{ik} for the goods measured monthly (m) or non-monthly (n) in city group i and month k, and set x_t, y_t, and z_t equal to sums of these. The months are indexed relative to the first month of the time period t. Thus if t indexes a quarter, m_{i1} indexes the first month of the quarter. Then the t index is again suppressed. The structure for the variances and covariances discussed in the text is as follows:

$$\left.\begin{array}{r} E(m_{ik}m_{jl}) \\ E(n_{ik}n_{jl}) \end{array}\right\} = \sigma_w^2 \begin{cases} 1 & i = j \text{ and } k = l \\ \omega & i \neq j \text{ but } k = l \\ \rho & \text{otherwise} \end{cases}$$

$$E(m_{ik}n_{jl}) = \sigma_w^2 \begin{cases} ck = l \\ ek \neq l \end{cases}$$

The monthly measurements before 1978 had the representation

$$x = \alpha_0 m_{01} + \alpha_1 m_{11} + \alpha_2 m_{21} + \alpha_3 m_{31} + \beta_0 n_{01}$$
$$y = \beta_1 n_{11} + \beta_2 n_{21} + \beta_3 n_{31}$$
$$z = \beta_1 n_{1-1} + \beta_1 n_{10} + \beta_1 n_{11}$$
$$\psi = \beta_1 n_{1-1} + \beta_1 n_{10} - \beta_2 n_{21} - \beta_3 n_{31}$$

The α_i and β_i represent the weights of the goods measured monthly and nonmonthly. The subscripts represent the four groups of cities. Since the weights of the groups of cities not measured nonmonthly are approximately equal, we simplify the algebra by

$$\alpha \equiv \alpha_1 = \alpha_2 = \alpha_3$$
$$\beta \equiv \beta_1 = \beta_2 = \beta_3$$

Then there results

$$E(\psi^2) = \beta^2 \sigma_w^2 2(1 + \rho - 2\rho) + 2(1 + \omega - 2\rho)$$
$$= \beta^2 \sigma_w^2 (4 + 2\omega - 6\rho)$$
$$E(d\psi) = -2\beta \sigma_w^2 \Big[\beta(1-\rho) + (2\beta+\beta_0)(\omega-\rho) + (3\alpha+\alpha_0)(c-e)\Big]$$
$$\sigma_d^2 = \sigma_w^2 \Big[\alpha_0(\alpha_0+3\alpha\omega+(\beta_0+3\beta)c) + \beta_0(\beta_0+3\beta\omega+(\alpha_0+3\alpha)c)$$
$$+ 3\alpha(\alpha+(\alpha_0+2\alpha)\omega+(\beta_0+3\beta)c) + 3\beta(\beta+(2\beta+\beta_0)\omega+(\alpha_0+3\alpha)c\Big]$$

Then with the central values $\rho = .3$, $\omega = .7$, $c = .26$, and $e = .22$, these equations give

$$\phi = \frac{-1}{\tau^2 + 2\tau\rho_{pw} + 1} /-15 + .13/.$$

Notice that the first term makes the sum negative and ϕ positive. This is the only error that gives a positive ϕ. This is typical for all six submodels. To understand this, set $z = 0$. Then we are estimating

$$q = a + b(p - x - y) + \epsilon$$
$$= a + b(p - x) + (\epsilon - by)$$

with an omitted variable.

If an omited variable is correlated positively with an included variable, the bias in the coefficient resulting is away from zero. The result differs from the formula for omission first obtained in that the weight of the correct portion is correct. Thus if in the first problem considered, $(1 - f)x$ were used instead of the correct $(1 - f)x + fy$, and if $\rho_{xy} > 0$, this would be an overcorrection moving the bias from toward zero to away from zero.

We now report the results of similar calculations for five other submodels. For quarterly models for pre-1978 we have (omitting the σ_w)

$$E(\psi^2) = \beta^2(6 + 4\omega - 10\rho)$$
$$E(d\psi) = -3\beta \Big[(\alpha_0+3\alpha)(c-e) + \beta(1-\rho)+(\beta_0+2\beta)(\omega-\rho)\Big]$$

and

$$\sigma_d^2 = 3\alpha_0 \Big[\alpha_0(1+2\rho) + 3\alpha(\omega+2\rho) + (\beta_0+3\beta)(c+2e)\Big]$$

$$+ 9\alpha \Big[\alpha_0(\omega+2\rho)+\alpha(1+2\rho)+2\alpha(\omega+2\rho)+(\beta_0+3\beta)(c+2e)\Big]$$

$$+ 3\beta_0 \Big[\beta_0(1+2\rho) + 3\beta(\omega+2\rho) + (\alpha_0+\alpha)(c+2e)\Big]$$

$$+ 9\beta \Big[\beta_0(\omega+2\rho)+\beta(1+2\rho)+2\beta(\omega+2\rho)+(\alpha_0+3\alpha)(c+2e)\Big]$$

For annual models for pre-1978, we have

$$E(\psi^2) = \beta^2 \Big[6 + 4\omega - 10\rho\Big]$$

$$E(d\psi) = -3\beta \Big[(\alpha_0 + 3\alpha)(c - e) + (\beta_0 + 2\beta)(\omega - \rho) + \beta(1 - \rho)\Big]$$

and

$$\sigma_d^2 = 12\alpha_0 \Big[\alpha_0(1+11\rho) + 3\alpha(\omega+11\rho) + (\beta_0+3\beta)(c+11e)\Big]$$

$$+ 36\alpha \Big[(\alpha_0+2\alpha)(\omega+11\rho)+\alpha(1+11\rho)+(\beta_0+3\beta)(c+11e)\Big]$$

$$+ 12\beta_0 \Big[\beta_0(1+11\rho) + 3\beta(\omega+11\rho) + (\alpha_0+3\alpha)(c+11e)\Big]$$

$$+ 36\beta \Big[(\beta_0+2\beta)(\omega+11\rho)+\beta(1+11\rho)+(\alpha_0+3\alpha)(c+11e)\Big]$$

For the period following the 1978 changes to the CPI, we reuse the symbols α and β. Where these denoted the weights for each of the three groups of cities measured nonmonthly in the older systems, they now denote the weights for each of the two groups of cities. For monthly regressions we have

$$E(\psi^2) = 2\beta^2(1 - \rho)$$

$$E(d\psi) = -\beta \Big[\beta(1-\rho) + (\beta_0+\beta)(\omega-\rho) + (\alpha_0+2\alpha)(c-e)\Big]$$

and

$$\sigma_d^2 = \alpha_0 \Big[\alpha_0+2\alpha\omega+(\beta_0+2\beta)c\Big] + 2\alpha \Big[\alpha+(\alpha_0+\alpha)\omega+(\beta_0+2\beta)c\Big]$$

$$+ \beta_0 \Big[\beta_0+2\beta\omega+(\alpha_0+2\alpha)c\Big] + 2\beta \Big[\beta+(\beta_0+\beta)\omega+(\alpha_0+2\alpha)c\Big]$$

For quarterly regressions we have

$$E(\psi^2) = 2\beta^2(1 - \rho)$$

$$E(d\psi) = -\beta \Big[\beta(1+\omega-2\rho) + \beta_0(\omega-\rho) + (\alpha_0+2\alpha)(c-e)\Big]$$

and

$$\sigma_d^2 = 3\alpha_0 \Big[\alpha_0(1+2\rho)+2\alpha(\omega+2\rho)+\beta_0(c+2e)+2\beta(c+2e)\Big]$$
$$+ 6\alpha \Big[\alpha(1+2\rho)+(\alpha_0+\alpha)(\omega+2\rho)+(\beta_0+2\beta)(c+2e)\Big]$$
$$+ 3\beta_0 \Big[\beta_0(1+2\rho)+2\beta(\omega+2\rho)+(\alpha_0+2\alpha)(c+2e)\Big]$$
$$+ 6\beta \Big[\beta(1+2\rho)(\beta_0+\beta)(\omega+2\rho)+(\alpha_0+2\alpha)(c+2e)\Big]$$

For annual regressions we have

$$E(\psi^2) = 2\beta(1 - \rho)$$
$$E(d\psi) = -\beta \Big[\beta_0(1-\rho)+\beta(1+\omega02\rho)+\alpha_0+2\alpha)(c-e)\Big].$$

and

$$E(d^2) = 12\alpha \Big[\alpha_0(1+11\rho)+2\alpha(\omega+11\rho)+(\beta_0+2\beta)(c+11e)\Big]$$
$$+ 24\alpha \Big[(\alpha_0+\alpha)(\omega+11\rho)+\alpha(1+11\rho)+(\beta_0+2\beta)(c+11e)\Big]$$
$$+ 12\beta_0 \Big[\beta_0(1+11\rho)+2\beta(\omega+11\rho)+(\alpha_0+2\alpha)(c+11e)\Big]$$
$$+ 24\beta \Big[\beta(1+11\rho)+(\beta_0+\beta)(\omega+11\rho)+(\alpha_0+2\alpha)(c+11e)\Big]$$

These are the equations used to calculate the effect of time period mismatches.

A.6 Combination Algorithms

The combination of different errors allows the possibility of many more parameters to estimate correlations between error terms. However, the simplest assumption of no correlations is reasonable for some of the errors. So we give the model for combining independent errors first.

We are assuming

$$w = d + \sum_{i=1}^{I} y_i$$

where $y_i, i = 1, \cdots, I$ are independent of each other and of d. These are useful assumptions for the errors due to sampling, quality, substitution, and dynamic effects. For each individual effect, we have estimated

$$\phi_i = cor(d, d + y_i) - 1$$

while we want the combined effect

$$\phi = cor(d, d + \sum_{i=1}^{I} y_i) - 1.$$

The individual correlations are

$$cor(d, d + y_i) = (1 + Var(y_i)/Var(d))^{-\frac{1}{2}}$$

and the combined correlation is

$$cor(d, d + \sum_{i=1}^{I} y_i) = (1 + \sum_{i=1}^{I} Var(y_i)/Var(d))^{-\frac{1}{2}}$$
$$= (1 + \sum_{i=1}^{I} (cor^{-2}(d, d + y_i) - 1))^{-\frac{1}{2}}$$

This is used to estimate the combined effect for the four errors mentioned and the result is designated ϕ_{ind}.

For the omission errors, we cannot assume independence between the true deflator and the error, so we examine a model with two omission errors. We take

$$d = (1 - f)(1 - g)w + fx + gy - fgz$$

Here w is used for estimation, x represents omitted goods for included consumers, y represents omitted consumers for included goods, and z represents omitted goods for omitted consumers. The fractions f and g are marginal fractions of goods and consumers omitted, as given in the text. It is assumed that the overlap is fg, which then enters with a negative sign since it has been counted twice. We assume, as previously, that all correlations with the nominal price are equal. For this discussion, we also take the denominator at its criterion value of 1. Then

$$-\phi = f(1 - \rho_{wx}) + g(1 - \rho_{wy}) - fg(1 - \rho_{wz})$$

One estimate for ρ_{wz} would be the minimum of ρ_{wx} and ρ_{wy}. A lower estimate would be their product. However, we use a cautious higher estimate, the average of the two. Then

$$-\phi = f(1 - g/2)(1 - \rho_{wx}) + g(1 - f/2)(1 - \rho_{wy})$$
$$\phi = (1 - g/2)\phi_{goods} + (1 - f/2)\phi_{consumers}$$

Housing and omitted time periods would require fairly detailed models for their combination. Because the effects are relatively small, however, they are simply added to the combined effects for omitted goods and consumers, and the result is denoted ϕ_{omit}.

It remains to combine the two groups. The following model with two different types of error is used. Take

$$d = (1 - f)e + fy$$

and

$$w = e + u$$

where u is independent of other variables and represents the errors that were combined independently, and y represents omitted portions. Then

$$-\phi = 1 - \rho_{dw}$$
$$= 1 - \left[(1 - f)\rho_{we} + f\rho_{we}\rho_{ey}\right]$$
$$= (1 - \rho_{we}) + \rho_{we}f(1 - \rho_{ey})$$

The first term is the fractional error due to u alone, and is identified as ϕ_{ind}. The second term contains the error from just omitting y, which is identified as the combination of omissions, ϕ_{omit}. The final combination is thus

$$\phi = \phi_{ind} + (1 + \phi_{ind})\phi_{omit}$$

B. Biases in Two Estimating Equations

Suppose

$$y_t = a + b\tilde{x}_t + u_t$$

while

$$x_t = \tilde{x}_t + v_t$$

and y_t are observed.
Let

$$X_t = \sum_{i=1}^{t} x_i$$
$$Y_t = \sum_{i=1}^{t} y_i$$

and

$$V_t = \sum_{i=1}^{t} v_i$$

We consider the two estimating equations

$$y_t = a_1 + b_1 x_t + r_t$$

and

$$Y_t = a_2 + b_2 X_t + R_t$$

where r_t and R_t are the residuals from the linear fits. We suppose that the distributions, denoted by "~(mean, variance)" are

$$u_t \sim (0, \sigma_u^2), \text{ independent of } \tilde{x}_t \text{ and } v_t$$
$$v_t \sim (0, \sigma_v^2)$$
$$\tilde{x}_t \sim (\mu\, \sigma_{\tilde{x}}^2)$$
$$cov(v_t \tilde{x}_s) = \delta_{ts} \rho_{\tilde{x}v}\, \sigma_{\tilde{x}} \sigma_v,$$

and

$$cov(\tilde{x}_t, \tilde{x}_s) = \sigma_{\tilde{x}}^2 \delta_{ts}$$

where

$$\delta_{ts} = \begin{cases} 1 & t = s \\ 0 & t \neq s \end{cases}$$

Also denote

$$var(x_t) = \sigma_{\tilde{x}}^2 + 2\rho_{\tilde{x}v}\, \sigma_{\tilde{x}} \sigma_v + \sigma_v^2$$
$$= \sigma_x^2$$

and

$$E(x_t v_t) \equiv \rho \sigma_x \sigma_v$$

Then the asymptotic fractional biases in b_1 and b_2 are

$$\phi_1 = -\lim_{T \to \infty} \frac{E[\frac{1}{T}\sum_{t=1}^{T}(x_t - \frac{1}{T}\sum_{s=1}^{T} x_s) v_t]}{E[\frac{1}{T}\sum_{t=1}^{T}(x_t - \frac{1}{T}\sum_{s=1}^{T} x_s)^2]}$$

and

$$\phi_2 = -\lim_{T \to \infty} \frac{E[\frac{1}{T}\sum_{t=1}^{T}(X_t - \frac{1}{T}\sum_{s=1}^{T} X_s) V_t]}{E[\frac{1}{T}\sum_{t=1}^{T}(X_t - \frac{1}{T}\sum_{s=1}^{T} X_s)^2]}$$

For ϕ_1 we have

$$E\left[\frac{1}{T}\sum_{t} = 1 x_t^2\right] = \frac{1}{T}\sum_{t=1}^{T}(\mu^2 + \sigma_x^2)$$

$$= \mu^2 + \sigma_x^2$$

and

$$E\left[\frac{1}{T}\sum_{t=1}^{T}x_t\right]^2 = \frac{1}{T^2}\sum_{t=1}^{T}\sum_{s=1}^{T}E(x_t x_s)$$

$$= \mu^2 + \frac{1}{T}\sigma_x^2$$

while

$$E\left[\frac{1}{T}\sum_{t=1}^{T}(x_t - \frac{1}{T}\sum_{s=1}^{T}x_s)v_t\right]$$

$$= \rho\,\sigma_x\,\sigma_v(1 - \frac{1}{T})$$

Thus

$$\phi_1 = \lim_{T\to\infty}\frac{(1 - \frac{1}{T})\rho\,\sigma_x\,\sigma_v}{(1 - \frac{1}{T})\sigma_x^2} = \frac{\rho\,\sigma_v}{\sigma_x}$$

This is well known, and is worked out here for consistency of notation with the calculation for ϕ_2. Here we have

$$E\left[\frac{1}{T}\sum_{t=1}^{T}(X_t)^2\right]$$

$$= \frac{(T+1)(2T+1)}{6}\mu^2 + T + \frac{1}{2}\sigma_x^2$$

and

$$E\left[\frac{1}{T}\sum_{t=1}^{T}X_t\right]^2$$

$$= \frac{(T+1)^2}{4}\mu^2 + \frac{(T+1)2T+1)}{6T}\sigma_x^2$$

We also have

$$E\left(\frac{1}{T}\sum_{t=1}^{T}(X_t - \frac{1}{T}\sum_{s=1}^{T}X_s)V_t\right)$$

$$= \rho\,\sigma_x\,\sigma_v\left\{\frac{1}{T}\sum_{t=1}^{T}t - \frac{1}{T^2}\sum_{t=1}^{T}\left[2\sum_{s=1}^{t-1}\sum_{i=1}^{s}1 + t\right]\right\}$$

$$= \rho\,\sigma_x\,\sigma_v\left\{T + \frac{1}{2} - \frac{1}{T^2}\sum_{t=1}^{T}t^2\right\}$$

$$= \rho\,\sigma_x\,\sigma_v\left\{T + \frac{1}{2} - (T+1)(2T+\frac{1)}{6T}\right\}$$

Thus there results for ϕ_2

$$\phi_2 = \lim_{T\to\infty}\frac{T\rho\,\sigma_x\,\sigma_v/6}{\mu^2 T^2/12 + \sigma_x^2 T/6}$$

$$= \lim_{T\to\infty}\frac{\rho\,\sigma_x\,\sigma_v}{T\mu^2/2 + \sigma_x^2}$$

For $\mu = 0$, $\phi_2 = \rho\sigma_v/\sigma_x = \phi_1$, while for $\mu \neq 0$, $\phi_2 = 0$.

What this appendix is showing is that if we are sure of a linear form of an equation, and if there is a trend in the data, then we really need only two points on the line to establish the slope, and so asymptotically we can measure this slope without bias. In the real world, we rarely have knowledge that an exactly linear relation holds, so using the summed form can lead to a false impression of how well the slope is measured. If there is no trend, however, the asymptotic bias is the same in either form.

References

Afriat, S. N. 1977. *The Price Index.* Cambridge, England: Cambridge University Press.

Andrews, David, P. J. Bickel, F. R. Hampel, P. J. Huber, W. H. Rogers, and J. W. Tukey. 1972. *Robust Estimates of Location.* Princeton, N.J.: Princeton University Press.

Braithwait, Steven D. 1975. "Consumer Demand and Cost of Living Indexes for the U.S.: An Empirical Comparison of Alternative Multi-level Demand Systems." Bureau of Labor Statistics Working Paper 45.

Cagan, Philip. 1966. "Measuring Quality Changes and the Purchasing Power of Money: An Exploratory Study of Automobiles." *National*

Banking Review. 3, pp. 217-236.

Christensen, Laurits R., and Marilyn E. Manser. 1974. "Cost of Living Indexes and Price Indexes for U.S. Meat and Produce,1947-1971." In N.E. Terleckyj, ed., *Conference on Household Production and Consumption, 1973, Washington.* National Bureau of Economic Research Series on Income and Wealth 40, New York: Columbia University Press.

DeMilner, Lawrence E. 1978 Speech given at Federal Statistics Users Conference on Inflation and Unemployment, Washington D.C.: October.

Devlin, Susan J., Ramanathan Gnanadesikan, and Jon R. Kettenring. 1975. "Robust Estimation and Outlier Detection with Correlation Coefficients." *Biometrika* 62, pp. 531-545.

Fama, Eugene F. 1975. "Short-Term Interest Rates as Predictors of Inflation," *American Economic Review* 65, pp. 269-282.

Fettig, Lyle P. 1963. "Adjusting Farm Tractor Prices for Quality Charges." *Journal of Farm Economics*, 45, pp. 599-611.

Fisher, Franklin, and Karl Shell. 1972. *The Economic Theory of Price Indices: Two Essays on the Effects of Taste, Quality, and Technological Change.* New York: Academic Press.

Gavett, Thomas W. 1967. "Research on Quality Adjustments in Price Indexes. Part III: Experiments on Multivariate Analysis of Quality Change." Unpublished BLS memorandum, Office of Prices and Living Conditions. Cited by Triplett (1977).

Griliches, Zvi. 1961. "Hedonic Price Indexes for Automobiles: An Econometric Analysis of Quality Change." Staff Paper Number 3 in Price Statistics Review Committee, *The Price Statistics of the Federal Government,* Washington, D.C., Government Printing Office.

Gutmann, Peter M. 1977. "The Subterranean Economy." *Financial Analysts Journal* (November/December 1977).

Johnston, J. 1972. *Econometric Methods,* 2nd ed. New York: McGraw-Hill.

Lloyd, P. J. 1975. "Substitution Effects and Biases in Nontrue Price Indices." *American Economic Review* 65, pp. 301-313.

Ohta, Makoto and Zvi Griliches. 1976. "Automobile Price Revisited: Extensions of the Hedonic Hypothesis." In N.E. Terleckyj, ed., *Conference on Household Production and Consumption, 1973, Washington.* National Bureau of Economic Research Series on Income and Wealth 40, New York: Columbia University Press.

Noe, Nicholas N., and George M. von Furstenberg. 1972. "The Upward Bias in the Consumer Price Index due to Substitution." *Journal of Political Economy.* 80, pp. 1280-1286.

Mosteller, Frederick, and John W. Tukey. 1977. *Data Analysis and Regression.* Reading, Mass.: Addison-Wesley.

Phlips, Louis. 1974. *Applied Consumption Analysis.* New York: Elsevier North-Holland.

Phlips, Louis, and Ricardo Sanz-Ferrer. 1975. "A Taste-Dependent True Index of the Cost of Living." *Review of Economics and Statistics* 57, pp. 495-501.

Rees, Albert. 1961. "Alternative Retail Price Indexes for Selected Non-Durable Goods." Staff Paper Number 2 in Price Statistics Review Committee, *The Price Statistics of the Federal Government.* Washington, D.C., Government Printing Office.

Triplett, Jack. 1971. "Quality Bias in Price Indexes and New Methods of Quality Measurement." In Zvi Griliches, ed., *Price Indexes and Quality Change.* Cambridge, Mass.: Harvard University Press.

Triplett, Jack. 1977. "The Measurement of Inflation: A Survey of Research on the Accuracy of Price Indexes." In Paul Earl, ed., *Analysis of Inflation.* Lexington, Mass.: Lexington Books.

Triplett, Jack E., and Richard J. McDonald. 1975. "Assessing the Quality Error in Output Measures: The Case of Refrigerators," Bureau of Labor Statistics Working Paper 37, published in *Review of Income and Wealth* (June 1977), pp. 137-156.

4

The International Economy as a Source of and Restraint on U.S. Inflation

Michael R. Darby

University of California, Los Angeles

1. Introduction

The balance of payments, changes in oil prices and other changes in our terms of trade, and other foreign influences are widely believed to be a major, if not the dominant, cause of inflation in the United States. This paper shows that such beliefs imply that the international economy influences the growth rate of the nominal quantity of money supplied or of the real quantity of money demanded, or both, in particular, testable ways. The postwar U.S. data are used to test these hypotheses. It is shown that the international economy has had at most trivial

The author acknowledges comments from William Gale, Arthur Gandolfi, James Lothian, and Anna Schwartz and generous support of the National Science Foundation (grant APR78-13072), the Relm Foundation, the Scaife Family Trusts, and the Alex C. Walker Foundation. Michael T. Melvin and Andrew A. Vogel provided able research assistance. The research reported here is part of the NBER's research program in International Studies. This article has not undergone the review accorded official NBER publications; in particular, it has not been submitted for approval by the Board of Directors and therefore is not a publication of the National Bureau.

effects on the average inflation rate over a period of four years or more. Although the effects of the international economy are negligible for U.S. inflationary trends, they may be significant for quarterly or even annual inflation rates and for inflationary trends in some other countries that maintained fixed exchange rates.

In Section 2, the inflation rate is shown to equal the difference between the growth rates of the nominal quantity of money supplied by the Federal Reserve System and of the real quantity of money demanded by the public. International influences on the behavior of the Federal Reserve System are examined in Section 3. International influences affect real money demand, particularly via changes in real income, but because these effects are once-and-for-all shifts their effect on the average inflation rate over four years is negligible, as seen in Section 4. Summary and conclusions are presented in Section 5.

2. Proximate Determinants of the Inflation Rate

The price level P states the amount of money that exchanges for a standard basket of goods and services. We call this basket — the average amounts bought with $1 in the arbitrary base year — a base-year dollar (B$), and the price level is measured as dollars per base-year dollar. The inverse of the price level, $1/P$ or the amount of goods per dollar, is the price or value of money. As with any commodity it is useful to organize our discussion of the determination of its price by examining the conditions of supply on the one hand and demand on the other.

The nominal quantity of money supplied M^S is the total amount of currency, coin, and checking deposits held by the public. It is measured in nominal or dollar amounts. Operating through the commercial banking system, our central bank, the Federal Reserve System ("the Fed"), determines M^S.

The nominal demand for money has the useful property of being homogeneous of degree 1 in the price level. That is, a doubling of the price level, other things equal, doubles the nominal quantity of money demanded. This is so because people are concerned with the real quantity of money measured in base-year dollars and not its nominal amount, whether it be measured in dollars or dimes or whatever. Thus, we normally write the nominal quantity of money demanded, M^d, as the product of the real quantity demanded, m^d, and the price level

$$M^d \equiv m^d P \qquad (4.1)$$

(The determinants of the real quantity of money demanded will be examined in detail in Section 4, with particular reference to channels of international influence.)

In equilibrium, the nominal quantities of money supplied and demanded must be equal, so substituting in (4.1) and solving for the price level:

$$P = \frac{M^S}{m^d} \qquad (4.2)$$

This equation states the price level in terms of the ratio of its proximate determinants: the nominal quantity of money supplied and the real quantity of money demanded.

We are concerned here with inflation, which is the growth rate of the price level. Let us define Γ_j as the growth rate operator such that

$$\Gamma_j X = \frac{\log X - \log X_{-j}}{j} \quad \text{for } any \ X > 0 \qquad (4.3)$$

where X_{-j} is the value of X j years previously. Thus Γ_j computes the continuously compounded growth rate per annum of a variable averaged over a period of j years. The j-year-average inflation rate $\Gamma_j P$ is, therefore,

$$\Gamma_j P = \Gamma_j M^S - \Gamma_j m^d \qquad (4.4)$$

The inflation rate is the difference between the average growth rates of the nominal quantity of money supplied and the real quantity of money demand over the same period.

For the observable nominal and real quantities of money, equation (4.4) is true by definition; the usefulness of the approach comes, from our ability to explain those quantities in terms of supply and demand conditions. Figure 4.1 illustrates the main channels by which the international economy might influence these supply and demand conditions. The balance of payments is hypothesized to influence the quantity of money that the Federal Reserve System chooses to supply. This influence has been observed for other countries that fix their exchange rate to the dollar, but this evidence is not necessarily applicable to a reserve-currency country like the United States. Factors that influence our terms of trade — such as the creation and decisions of OPEC — affect our real income, which is a major determinant of the real quantity of money demand. We must examine empirically whether these

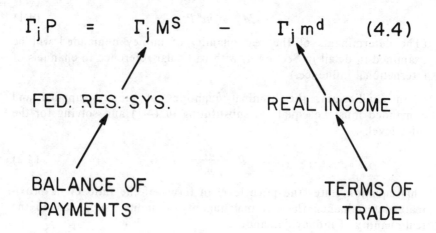

Figure 4.1
Channels for International Influences

factors have had a sufficiently large impact to cause significant variations in the growth rate of the real quantity of money demand.

The general equilibrium approach embodied in equation (4.4) elucidates the error in the partial equilibrium, or adding-up, approach. This latter approach explains the inflation rate as a weighted sum of the inflation rates of individual goods and services without due allowance for the adjustment of wages, profits, and rents to make equation (4.4) hold. That is, the partial equilibrium approach starts from the definition of the price level as a weighted sum of the prices P_a of m commodities identified by the subscript a:

$$P \equiv \sum_{i=1}^{m} w_i P_a \qquad (4.5)$$

For growth rates, the following formula therefore holds approximately:

$$\Gamma_j P = \sum_{a=1}^{m} \frac{w_a P_a}{P} \Gamma_j P_a \qquad (4.6)$$

The argument goes that a rapid increase in the price of an individual commodity, such as oil, contributes to inflation according to its weight $\frac{w_a P_a}{P}$ plus any induced increase in other prices of closely related products. The problem with the approach is that it ignores the small but pervasive downward effect on the prices of all other commodities so that the general equilibrium condition (4.4) holds. Factors that make one particular group of prices rise more rapidly influence the *average* growth rate of prices only to the extent that they increase the growth of the nominal money supply or reduce the growth rate of real money demanded.

3. Determinants of Nominal Money Supply Growth

The Federal Reserve System, a semi-independent agency within the legislative branch of government, operates through the commercial banking system to control the nominal quantity of money. Among the factors that influence the Fed's behavior are recent inflation and unemployment rates and unexpected changes in government expenditure. The first two factors are relevant to the Fed's role in attempting to stabilize, while the third factor refers to the central bank's traditional financing of unexpected government expenditures by resort to the printing press.

A general behavioral function describing the nominal money supply behavior of the central bank is drawn from the Mark III International

Transmission Model[1] and reproduced here:[2]

$$\Delta \log M = \underset{\substack{(0.003) \\ 1.59}}{0.004} + \underset{\substack{(0.12) \\ 3.98}}{0.461} \, \Delta \log M_{-1} - \underset{\substack{(0.12) \\ -1.98}}{0.230} \, \Delta \log M_{-2} + \underset{\substack{(0.00005) \\ 5.06}}{0.00025} \, t$$

$$+ \underset{\substack{(0.029) \\ 0.14}}{0.004} \, \hat{g} + \underset{\substack{(0.021) \\ 0.08}}{0.002} \, (\hat{g}_{-1} + \hat{g}_{-2}) + \underset{\substack{(0.020) \\ 1.46}}{0.029} \, (\hat{g}_{-3} + \hat{g}_{-4})$$

$$- \underset{\substack{(0.090) \\ -0.64}}{0.058} \, (\log P_{-1} - \log P_{-3}) - \underset{\substack{(0.100) \\ -2.38}}{0.237} \, (\log P_{-3} - \log P_{-5})$$

$$- \underset{\substack{(0.193) \\ -0.60}}{0.117} \, u_{-1} + \underset{\substack{(0.363) \\ 1.49}}{0.539} \, u_{-2} - \underset{\substack{(0.367) \\ -1.18}}{0.432} \, u_{-3} - \underset{\substack{(0.195) \\ -0.28}}{0.055} \, u_{-4} \qquad (4.7)$$

$$\bar{R}^2 = 0.56, \quad S.E.E. = 0.0046, \quad D-W = 2.05$$

The estimation is based on quarterly data for 1957-I through 1976-IV. The notation is t for time in quarters, $\hat{g}$ for unexpected real government expenditures, P for the GNP deflator, u for the unemployment rate, and the negative subscripts indicate lags in quarters. The regression explains 56 percent of the quarterly variation in the growth rate of money, although the policy response to government spending, inflation, and unemployment is relatively weak and a long time coming. Beta coefficients (presented in Table 4.1) normalize the variables by their standard deviations and serve to indicate the relative contributions of the variables to variation in nominal money growth. They confirm the impression gained from examining the coefficients and t-statistics. Note that a great deal is hidden in the trend term, which implies a gradual increase in the steady-state growth rate of nominal money from .2 percent per annum at the end of 1956 to 6.0 percent per annum at the end of 1976.[3] Indeed, a constant and the time trend alone would

---

1. See Darby and Stockman (1980).

2. The standard errors appear below the coefficients in parentheses, and t-values appear below the standard errors. The estimation was by two-stage least squares using principal components of the predetermined variables in the Mark III model. Durbin's h cannot be computed in this case.

3. This steady-state growth assumes all variables equal their expected values: $\hat{g} = \hat{g}_{-1} = \hat{g}_{-2} = \hat{g}_{-3} = \hat{g}_{-4} = 0$, $\log P_{-1} - \log P_{-3} = \log M_{-1} - \log M_{-3} - \frac{1}{2}\mu$, $\log P_{-3} - \log P_{-5} = \log M_{-3} - \log M_{-1} - \frac{1}{2}\mu$, $u_{-1} = u_{-2} = u_{-3} = u_{-4} = \bar{u}$, where μ is the steady-state growth rate of real money (see Section 3) and $\bar{u}$, the natural rate of unemployment, is .0475 in 1956 and .0575 in 1976. The precise values of the

TABLE 4.1

Beta Coefficients for the Nominal Supply Reaction Function (4.7)

Variable	Beta Coefficient
$\Delta \log M_{-1}$	0.461
$\Delta \log M_{-2}$	−0.232
t	0.841
$\hat{g}$	0.011
$\hat{g}_{-1} + \hat{g}_{-2}$	0.006
$\hat{g}_{-3} + \hat{g}_{-4}$	0.118
$\log P_{-1} - \log P_{-3}$	−0.104
$\log P_{-3} - \log P_{-5}$	−0.426
u_{-1}	−0.220
u_{-2}	1.000
u_{-3}	−0.789
u_{-4}	−0.098

Notes: Beta coefficients are one measure of the relative contributions of the independent variables to the variability of the dependent variable. They are equal to the ratio of (a) the coefficient times the standard deviation of the independent variable to (b) the standard deviation of the dependent variable.

explain approximately 31 percent of the quarterly variation in the dependent variable, with all the other variables explaining only an additional 25 percent. We shall return to this later.

A great many countries choose to fix their exchange rate with some other currency. This requires that they adjust nominal money growth to their balance of payments. This is not true for a fiat reserve country such as the United States,[4] but it is worthwhile to check whether the Federal Reserve System in fact responded to the balance of payments. To test this, I added three terms B, $(B_{-1} + B_{-2})$, and $(B_{-3} + B_{-4})$ to equation (4.7), where B is the ratio of the balance of payments to income. All three coefficients were very small and of the wrong sign. Also, the standard error of the regression rose and the corrected R^2 fell. The formal test for all three coefficients being equal to zero yielded an $F(3/64)$ statistic of only .26 compared to a 95-percent critical value of 2.75. Thus the evidence strongly indicates that international factors have not affected U.S. nominal money growth via the balance of payments.

Absent the main channel by which international factors affect the nominal money supply in nonreserve countries, we must consider indirect effects. The existence of temporary effects on the inflation rate or unemployment rate would bring about a temporary effect on the growth rate of the nominal money supply. Possibly some of the unaccounted-for variance could result from Fed responses to international factors that are uncorrelated with the balance of payments, but these factors are apparently serially uncorrelated and therefore not a source of a continuing effect of the nominal quantity of money supplied.

Summarizing, as appropriate for a reserve country, the balance of payments has had no effect on U.S. nominal money growth. No other channel would appear to offer any possibility for other than temporary effects on nominal money growth from the international sector.

The central bank's reaction function (4.7) mainly labels our ignorances to the cause of the upward trend in nominal money growth. It has been widely supposed that printing money to finance the Vietnam War began the process. However, neither the fraction of the total labor force in the military nor the number of troops in Vietnam, when added

---

natural unemployment rate are not important to these calculations and the 4 3/4 and 5 3/4 percent figures are my approximations of the mean estimates in the literature.

4. See Darby (1980). A fiat reserve country is one that does not attempt to maintain a pegged exchange rate and that issues inconvertible paper money.

to reaction function (4.7) enter at all significantly.[5] In each regression, including the Vietnam variable reduced the corrected R^2 and increased the standard error of the regression. Thus the Vietnam War apparently had no more effect than would be implied by any similar series of unexpected increases in government spending. If the upward trend reflects a gradual increase in the acceptable level of inflation as a result of our experience, perhaps the Vietnam War was indeed the beginning of the process, which has since fed on itself.

4. Determinants of Real Money Demand Growth

The demand for money is one of the most thoroughly investigated topics in economics.[6] There are a number of variations, but the main theme is that the real quantity of money demanded m^d is a stable function of the nominal interest rate r and total real income y. In the short run, unexpected changes in the growth rate of the nominal quantity of money supplied induce movements in r and y that in turn change the growth rate of real money demand by the same amount. However, it is argued that these changes in r and y are temporary, and in the long run all the effects are on prices with the real quantity of money demanded returning to its original growth path.[7]

Changes in our terms of trade can affect the real quantity of money demanded and hence the price level in two distinct ways — one transitory and one permanent. The temporary effect occurs because an unexpected adverse change (an OPEC price increase, say) will shift up the supply curve of tradable goods immediately while it takes time for the adjustments in domestic factor prices to occur, as discussed at the end of Section 1. Figure 4.2 illustrates how a temporary upward shift in the aggregate supply curve from AS to AS' would cause a temporary fall in real income from $\bar{y}$ to y' and a rise in the price level from $\bar{P}$ to P'. But these temporary effects are self-reversing as factor prices adjust and unemployment falls back toward its normal level.

Permanent effects of changes in the terms of trade on the real demand for money (and so the price level) would arise from permanent changes in the steady-state (long-run equilibrium) growth paths of real

---

5. Distributed lags of the military variables alone or in combination with the balance-of-payments variables also failed to enter.

6. Standard reviews of the literature are Laidler (1977, 1980) and Goldfeld (1973). The author's own views are reported in Darby (1979) and Carr and Darby (1981).

7. This holds strictly only in the case of superneutrality; we proceed on the assumption that this case holds sufficiently well for empirical work. See Darby (1979, pp. 134-137, 207-213) for analysis for the nonsuperneutral case.

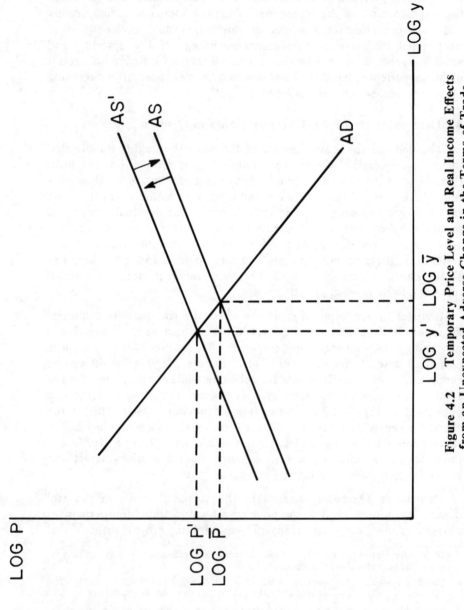

Figure 4.2   Temporary Price Level and Real Income Effects
from an Unexpected Adverse Change in the Terms of Trade

income or the interest rate. Some economists[8] have argued that the change in U.S. terms of trade associated with the creation of OPEC reduced real income permanently by as much as 3 to 5 percent. I would argue that those estimates are on the high side because price controls, which caused an overstatement of real income in the official data, were coincidentally removed.[9] Be that as it may, note that this is a permanent once-and-for-all reduction in the *level* of real income and not a permanent reduction in its *growth rate*. Figure 4.3 illustrates such a once-and-for-all percentage reduction in log m^d at time t for a given constant growth rate of the nominal quantity of money supplied. An equal once-and-for-all percentage increase in the price level is implied. Note that the average inflation rate (the slope of log P) is affected only for observations including time t.

Suppose that μ is the normal growth rate in the real quantity of money demanded due to normal growth in real income and the interest rate plus any technological change in payments technology and institutions. Any one once-and-for-all decrease in real income reduces real money demand but does not affect μ.

$$\Gamma_j m^d = \mu + \frac{1}{j} \sum_{i=0}^{j-1} \epsilon_{-1} \qquad (4.8)$$

Assuming that these shifts are uncorrelated with mean 0, the mean value of $\Gamma_j m^d$ is μ and the variance is σ^2/j where σ^2 is the variance of ϵ. Whether the actual stochastic distribution of the ϵ's is such (i.e., sufficiently ergodic) that the variance of $\Gamma_j m^d$ becomes trivial in a reasonably short period is an empirical question. If so, even though these shifts in the level of real money demand do cause once-and-for-all price level shifts, the average effect of these price level shifts is negligible in discussing inflation trends.

To illustrate this empirically, I estimate the regression

$$\Gamma_j P = \Gamma_j M - \mu - \epsilon \qquad (4.9)$$

for alternative observation lengths j. This ϵ includes not only the effects of once-and-for-all shifts in real money demand but also temporary induced movements in money demand. Since the induced movements are self-reversing and hence strongly ergodic, they too

---

8. Notably Rasche and Tatom (1977) and Mork and Hall (1979).

9. See Darby (1976). The real price of oil had one sharp upward movement during our sample period (1973-1974) with a mild downward trend both before and afterwards. A second movement occurring at this writing (1979-1980) may ultimately allow us to differentiate the oil-price effects from the price-control effects in 1973-1974.

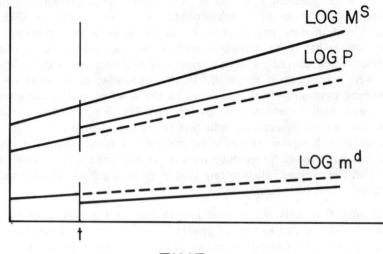

TIME

NOTE : LOG P = LOG M^S − LOG m^d

Figure 4.3
Once-and-for-all Shift in m^d at Time t

average out for longer sample periods. Table 4.2 lists the standard errors, corrected R^2s and Durbin-Watson statistics on the M_1 definition of money for data from 1954-IV through 1978-IV.[10] For quarterly data, nominal money does not help predict the inflation rate.[11] For annual and biennial data, we get improvement but still have substantial unexplained variance. With quadrennial data, however, the standard error of the residuals from the inflation rate drops to about 1 percent per annum and the unexplained variance drops to around 19 percent. (A positive $\overline{R}^2$ can be interpreted as the fraction of the dependent variable's variance, which is explained by the regression.) Thus, while shifts in real money demand play a substantial role in short-run inflationary developments, long-run inflation trends are dominated by movements in the average growth rate of the nominal quantity of money supplied.

Some of these variations in the growth rate of the real quantity of money demanded are caused by the variations in the growth rate of the nominal quantity supplied, as noted at the beginning of this section. We can get an idea of how much variation in the growth rate of real money demand is due to autonomous (non-money-supply) forces by regressing the current inflation rate on current and lagged nominal money growth:

$$\Gamma_j P = \sum_{i=0}^{4/j} k_i \Gamma_m M_{-ij} - \mu - \epsilon \qquad (4.10)$$

The four-year-distributed lag on money growth appears sufficient from the previous work of others to allow for most of the effects of variations in nominal money growth on the growth rate of real money demand.[12] Table 4.3 reports regression estimates of equation (4.10). We see by comparison with Table 4.2 that about half of the standard error of the growth rate of real money demand is due to variations in the growth rate of nominal money supply. That is, the ratio of the standard error in Table 4.3 to that in Table 4.2 is .56 for quarterly observations and .52, .6, and .42 for annual, biennial, and quadrennial

---

10. I started in 1954 to avoid the Korean War price controls, and 1978 is the last full year of data available at the time of writing.

11. It would if the constraint that the coefficients of $\Gamma_j M = 1$ were not imposed. The negative corrected $\overline{R}^2$ is telling us that the variance in the quarterly growth rate of real money is greater than that of the quarterly inflation rate.

12. Note that there are sixteen lag terms when $j = 1/4$ and only one lag term when $j = 4$. This is obviously not a model that will maximize the explanatory power of nominal money growth for the inflation rate, but it should provide a good lower bound for the $\overline{R}^2$.

TABLE 4.2

Summary Statistics for Prediction of Inflation Rates, $\Gamma_j P$, as $\Gamma_j M - \mu$

Observation Length (j)	S.E.E.	$\bar{R}^2$	D-W
1/4 year	.0291	−.2547	.74
1 year	.0229	.1045	1.46
2 years	.0189	.3455	2.29
4 years	.0095	.8078	1.21

Notes: P is the GNP deflator; M is the M_1 (currency + demand deposits) money stock; all regressions are run on data from 1954-IV through 1978-IV.

TABLE 4.3

Summary Statistics for Prediction of Inflation

$$\text{Rates by } \Gamma_j P = \sum_{i=0}^{4/j} k_i \Gamma_j M_{-ij} - \mu$$

Observation Length (j)	S.E.E.	$\overline{R}^2$	D-W
1/4 year	.0165	.6264	1.00
1 year	.0119	.7802	1.48
2 years	.0121	.7586	1.74
4 years	.0040	.9699	2.83

Notes: P is the GNP deflator; M is the M_1 (currency + demand deposits) money stock; all regressions are run for 1958-IV through 1978-IV on data from 1954-IV through 1978-IV.

observations, respectively. Indeed, current and lagged growth rates of nominal money alone explain about 60 percent of the variance of quarterly inflation rates, 75 percent for annual and biennial inflation rates, and over 95 percent of the variance of quadrennial inflation rates. Since the total unexplained variance due to both domestic and international sources of variation in the growth of real money demand is so small, I conclude that as an empirical matter the international economy has had a negligible influence via the real money demand channel.

5. Conclusions and Summary

This discussion has been organized in terms of the proximate determinants of the inflation rate: the average growth rates of nominal money supply and real money demand.

The balance of payments has a powerful effect on the money supply of countries that maintain fixed exchange rates. This need not be the case for a fiat reserve country such as the United States, and no balance-of-payments effect on U.S. monetary policy was detected empirically. Thus the international economy could affect the growth rate of nominal quantity of money supplied only through temporary and indirect channels.

Effects on real money demand due to changes in real income appeared plausible. On theoretical grounds, however these effects are either self-reversing and temporary or once-and-for-all and result in price level shifts that again only temporarily affect the inflation rate. Empirically, these expectations are supported because most of the variation in inflation rates is explained by variations in the growth rate of the nominal quantity of money supplied even for quarterly or annual observations. Measuring inflationary trends by quadrennial averages, over 95 percent of the variance in inflation is explained by nominal money (M_1) growth rates, with less than 5 percent attributable to autonomous movements in the growth rate of the real quantity of money demanded due to both domestic and international factors. Thus the long-run influence of international factors on the U.S. inflation rate is negligible, although such factors may play a supporting role in the short run.

This negative conclusion leaves the responsibility for U.S. inflationary trends squarely on the Federal Reserve System. The international economy cannot be blamed for our poor performance to date nor used to excuse future failures.

References

Carr, Jack, and Michael R. Darby. 1981. "The Role of Money Supply Shocks in the Short-Run Demand for Money." *Journal of Monetary Economics* (forthcoming).

Darby, Michael R. 1976. "The U.S. Economic Stabilization Program of 1971-1974." In Michael Walker, ed., *The Illusion of Wage and Price Control*. Vancouver: The Fraser Institute.

Darby, Michael R. 1976. *Intermediate Macroeconomics*. New York: McGraw-Hill.

Darby, Michael R. 1980. "The Monetary Approach to the Balance of Payments: Two Specious Assumptions." *Economic Inquiry* 18 (1980), pp. 321-326.

Darby, Michael R., and Alan C. Stockman. 1980. "The Mark III International Transmission Model." National Bureau of Economic Research Working Paper No. 42, February.

Goldfeld, Stephen M. 1973. "The Demand for Money Revisited." *Brookings Papers on Economic Activity*, No. 3, pp. 577-638.

Laidler, David E. W. 1977. *The Demand for Money: Theories and Evidence* 2nd ed. New York: Donnelley.

Laidler, David E. W. 1980. "The Demand for Money in the United States Yet Again." In K. Brunner and A. H. Meltzer, eds. *On the States of Macroeconomics*. Carnegie-Rochester Conference Series on Public Policy, vol. 12.

Mork, Knut A., and Robert E. Hall. 1980. "Energy Prices, Inflation, and Recession, 1974-1975." *The Energy Journal* 1, No. 3 (July), pp. 31-63.

Rasche, Robert H., and John A. Tatom. 1977. "The Effects of the New Energy Regime on Economic Capacity, Production, and Prices." *Federal Reserve Bank of St. Louis Review* 59, No. 5 (May), pp. 2-12.

5

Why the Great Inflation Has Been a Catastrophe

Paul Evans
Stanford University

1. Introduction

Most Americans regard inflation as Public Enemy Number 1.[1] In contrast, many economists have difficulty understanding why inflation poses any important problems. In fact, some economists[2] have argued that the public's negative attitude toward inflation may be an illusion. According to this view, a rapid inflation, which by definition is a rapid rise in the prices of all goods in the economy, results in a rapid rise in each person's income. Each person, however, firmly believes that the rapid rise in his own income is due to his own virtue while equally firmly believing that the prices of the goods he buys rise because of profiteers and greedy unions. If the inflation rate could just be held down somewhat, he thinks, the rapid rise in his income would enable him to raise his standard of living rapidly.

There is some evidence that this illusion is at least in part responsible for the public's antipathy toward inflation.[3] To the extent that this illusion is the sole reason why the public cries out against inflation, it

---

1. See the polls published in *Public Opinion*, May/June 1978, pp. 30-32.
2. For example, Fischer and Modigliani (1978).
3. Ibid.

would be wise for policymakers to ignore this outcry.

This paper, however, takes the view that the public has objective reasons to dislike inflation. It shows that, given the institutional structure of the U.S. economy, inflation during the period 1972-1980[4] has led to a lower growth rate and to social costs that may be as large as the current national income. If inflation continues at its current rate and the institutional structure remains unchanged, the growth rate will continue to be depressed and the social loss will be markedly higher.

2. Inflation and Relative Prices

A central proposition in economics is that economic decisions are based solely on *relative* prices. Relative prices tell consumers which goods to buy. They tell producers which goods to produce and how to produce those goods. In the process, they determine the rewards that accrue to individuals for their productive activities. The *absolute* price of a good, which is the number of intrinsically worthless pieces of green paper that a person must give up to get one unit of that good, is of no significance because no one cares about how many pieces of green paper he receives for what he sells or how many pieces of green paper he must pay for what he buys. Economic agents care only about how many of the things they sell must be given up in order to get the things that they buy.

This proposition has the following important corollary:
> *If all economic agents in the economy always adjust completely, a perfectly anticipated inflation has no effects on the economy, however great its rate may be.*

It is easy to see why this corollary is true. Suppose that every absolute price exactly doubles. No relative price changes. Exactly the same goods are produced and consumed, using the same techniques of production, and they are distributed exactly as they were before the price level doubled. Now, suppose that the price level doubles over some period of time. The relative prices at the end of the period are exactly the same as they would have been if the price level had not doubled. Since the length of the period is arbitrary, it follows that the inflation rate does not affect the economy.

This corollary depends on two important qualifications. First, the inflation rate must be perfectly anticipated. By perfectly anticipated, I mean that all economic agents must always forecast the inflation rate

---

4. I shall somewhat flamboyantly call this period the Great Inflation.

perfectly and must base their economic decisions on these forecasts. Second, all economic agents must always adjust completely. If either of these conditions is violated, inflation will affect what is produced, how it is produced, and who gets the products.

Inflation has never been perfectly anticipated, and it never shall be, as Carlson discusses in this volume. Furthermore, many economic agents fail to adjust completely to inflation. In this paper, I neglect the effects of unanticipated inflation, focusing instead on incomplete adjustment. I further limit the analysis to the failure of a single agent in the U.S. economy to adjust to inflation. This agent, the federal government, is by far the most important agent in the U.S. economy. In the next section, I show that the federal government has allowed the inflation rate to affect its tax rates. I then show that this behavioral pattern has important effects on the U.S. economy. To be specific, it has appreciably retarded the growth of the U.S. economy and has led to a large social loss.

3. The Tax Laws

The federal government bases its tax code on accounting rules that are valid only if the price level is constant. When there is inflation, the tax rates on most types of real income change even when no one's real income has changed. Since tax rates affect the relative prices in the economy, a change in the inflation rate will change what is produced, how it is produced, and who gets the products unless the federal government changes its tax code in the interim to prevent this from happening.

Inflation affects the individual tax rates in several ways. The one on which I shall concentrate is the moving of taxpayers into higher income tax brackets. For example, consider a married couple filing a joint. return and reporting $28,000 in net taxable income in 1979. This couple would pay $4505 plus 32 percent of the difference between $28,000 and $24,000. They pay a marginal federal income tax rate on net taxable income[5] of 32 percent because earning an additional $100 of net taxable income would result in $32 more in federal income taxes. Note that this tax rate is relevant for economic decisionmaking because it affects after-tax relative prices.

Now, suppose that the price level rises 10 percent. The couple finds itself with $30,800 in net taxable income[6] and therefore in the

---

5. The marginal federal tax rate on total income is somewhat lower because households generate more deductions as their incomes rise.

$29,900-$35,000 bracket. They must pay a marginal tax rate of 37 percent even though their net taxable income does not permit them to buy any more goods than they used to buy. This change in the marginal tax rate will lead the couple to change their behavior and will thus change what is produced, how it is produced, and who gets it.

If the federal government wanted to prevent inflation from affecting marginal tax rates, it would have to index its tax code. Basically, indexing requires that taxes be levied only on real income. The major change necessary in the personal income tax code would be to make every nominal magnitude proportional to the price level. For example, the three bracket amounts and the dollar tax payment mentioned above would rise by 10 percent when the price level rose by 10 percent.

To illustrate how inflation has actually affected the marginal tax rate, I have plotted in Figure 5.1 the tax rate imposed by the federal government on ordinary income for each of the years between 1970 and 1978.[7] Between 1970 and 1972, the consumer price index rose 3.7 percent per year,[8] and the marginal federal income tax rate rose only .2 percentage points per year. Since then — in the period of Great Inflation — the consumer price index has risen 7.4 percent per year, and the marginal federal income tax rate has risen 1.0 percentage points per year. In only one year since 1972 has the consumer price index risen less than 6 percent per year. That year, 1976, is the only year in which the marginal federal income tax rate fell.

It is hard to believe that the marginal federal income tax rate would have risen as rapidly as it did between 1972 and 1978 if Congress had been forced to legislate an increase in statutory tax rates to achieve this result. Indeed, Congress actually lowered statutory tax rates, but rapid inflation converted these de jure reductions into de facto increases. I conclude that inflation produces a rising marginal federal income tax rate. In other words, the federal government does not adjust completely to inflation.

To estimate the extent to which the the federal government fails to adjust to inflation, I have regressed changes in the marginal federal income tax rate on the rate of inflation, obtaining the following result:[9]

---

6. Actually, deductions may not rise by exactly 10 percent, so this statement is only approximately true.

7. This marginal tax rate is the average of the marginal tax rates paid by eleven income classes. These marginal tax rates take into account the effects of income on deductions. I have taken these data from Ranson et al. (1979).

8. See the 1977 *Business Statistics* and the November 1979 *Survey of Current Business*.

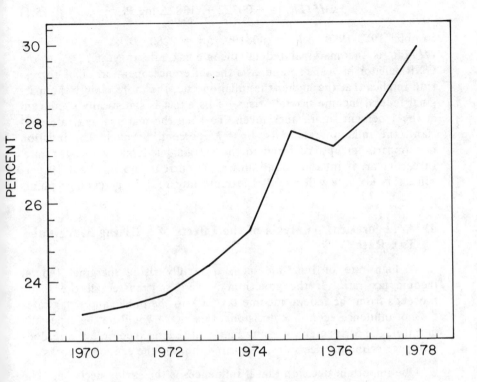

Figure 5.1
The Marginal Federal Income Tax Rate of the United States

$$\Delta MFITR_t = -.00322 + .1882\Delta \log P_t . \qquad (5.1)$$
$$(.00307)(.0707)$$

Sample: 1953-1978, *S.E.* = .008199, R^2 = .2280, *D.W.* = 1.94, where
$MFITR_t$ is the marginal federal income tax rate in year t, P_t is the
GNP deflator in year t,[10] and Δ is the difference operator. This regression
implies that the higher the inflation rate, the more rapidly the marginal federal income tax rate rises. This effect is statistically significant
at the 1 percent significance level. To keep the marginal tax rate constant, the inflation rate must be 1.72 percent.[11] Any higher inflation
rate imparts an upward trend to the marginal federal income tax rate.
In particular, if inflation continues at its current rate of about 10 percent, this tax rate will rise at the rapid rate of 1.56 percentage points
per year.

4. A Theoretical Analysis of the Effects of a Rising Marginal Tax Rate

A high rate of inflation spells a rapidly rising marginal federal
income tax rate. If the government were to transfer all the rising
proceeds from the federal income tax back to the public and if tax rates
did not influence economic decisions, this effect would not be especially
harmful. Unfortunately, a rising marginal federal income tax rate does
influence economic decisions, distorting the way the economy works.

One important decision that it influences is the saving decision. The
higher the marginal federal income tax rate will be in the future, the
less each individual can consume in the future for any given sacrifice of
current consumption and hence the less each individual can save. Less
saving results in more consumption now; however, because the capital
stock and hence output will be lower at each future date, consumption
will eventually be reduced.

If there are no distortions in the private economy affecting the saving decision, this shift in consumption from the future to the present
gives rise to a social loss. To see why, examine Figure 5.2. Without
loss of generality, I simplify the analysis by considering only two
periods, $t-1$ and t, and by assuming that the tax rate on income in
period t is initially zero. *AB* is the locus of consumption that is

9. The figures in parentheses are standard errors.
10. The data, which are annual, come from Ranson et al. (1979), the *National Income and Product Accounts*, and the *Survey of Current Business*.
11. This point estimate, which equals .00322/.1882, is subject to considerable sampling error.

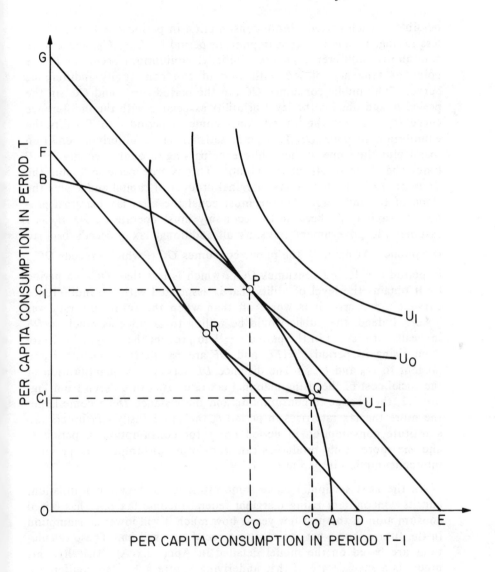

Figure 5.2
Distortion of the Saving Decision

possible in each period. More consumption in period $t - 1$, and hence less saving, entails less consumption in period t. U_{-1}, U_0, and U_1 are community indifference curves. Initially, equilibrium occurs at P, the point of tangency of AB with one of the community indifference curves. The public consumes OC_0 in the period $t - 1$ and OC_1 in the period t, and obtains the level of utility associated with the indifference curve U_0. Raising the tax rate on income in period t to T shifts the equilibrium to point Q. This point satisfies the equilibrium condition that 1 plus the slope of the indifference passing through it equals $1 - T$ times the slope of AB at the point.[12] This is true because 1 plus the slope of AB is the before-tax marginal product of capital and 1 plus the slope of the indifference curve must equal the after-tax marginal product of capital and because the economy must operate on AB if, as I assume, the government transfers all additional tax proceeds back to the public. At point Q, the public consumes OC_0', which exceeds OC_0, in period $t - 1$, and consumes OC_1', which is less than OC_1, in period t. It obtains the level of utility that is associated with the indifference curve U_{-1}; clearly, it is worse off than when the future tax rate was lower. Indeed, the public would be willing to sacrifice as much as DE in wealth or income in the period $t - 1$ to prevent the marginal tax rate from rising in period t. (EG and DF are parallel to each other and tangent to U_0 and U_{-1}.) The distance DE serves as a quantification of the social cost of the rising marginal tax rate. As can be seen from Figure 5.2, the change in consumption and the distance DE become larger the more the tax rate rises in period t, the more easily consumers can substitute consumption in period $t - 1$ for consumption in period t, and the more easily producers can transform consumption in period t into consumption in period $t - 1$.

In the next section, I make some estimates of how much inflation, and its concomitant rising marginal federal income tax rate, has raised consumption in the past few years, how much it will lower consumption in the future, and what the resulting social cost will be. These calculations are based on the model detailed in Appendix A. Basically, this model is a special case of that underlying Figure 5.2. The indifference curves are assumed to have the slope[13]

---

12. This condition holds if there is no population growth. The condition becomes somewhat more complicated if the population is growing.

13. Note that (5.2) is the simplest possible expression for the slope that assigns arbitrary values to both the slope and curvature of the indifference curves.

$$- (1 + r)(C_t/C_{t-1})^e \quad t = 2,3,..., \tag{5.2}$$

where C_{t-1} and C_t are the per-capita consumptions in periods $t - 1$ and t, and r and e are positive parameters. The parameter r measures the public's time preference; it is the marginal product of capital net of replacement and taxes that would prevail if per-capita consumption were constant. The parameter e measures the substitutability of current and future consumption. The larger e is, the less substitutable current and future consumption are. For example, when $e = 0$, the indifference curves in Figure 5.2 are straight lines and consumption is perfectly substitutable across time; and when $e = \infty$, the indifference curves in Figure 5.2 are rectangles with their corners on the $C_t = C_{t-1}$ line and consumption is not substitutable at all across periods.

The consumption-possibility frontier is defined implicitly by the intertemporal budget constraint, which I assume to be

$$C_t = b(1 + a)^{(1-s)t}K_t^s - (K_{t+1} - K_t) - nK_{t+1} - dK_t - G_t \tag{5.3}$$

where K_t and K_{t+1} are the per-capita stocks in periods t and $t + 1$; G_t is per-capita government purchases; a, n, and d are the exogenous rates of technological growth, population growth, and depreciation of capital; and s is the share of capital in gross income. The term $(1 + a)^{(1-s)t}K_t^s$ is per-capita gross output; the assumption here is that output is produced according to a linear homogeneous Cobb-Douglas technology.[14] To obtain per-capita consumption, we must subtract from per-capita gross output $K_{t+1} - K_t$, the per-capita increment in the per-capita capital stock; nK_{t+1}, the per-capita investment necessary to equip next period's new population with K_{t+1} per-capita capital; dK_t, the per-capita investment necessary to replace used capital; and G_t, per-capita absorption of output by the government.

To determine what the slope of the consumptions-possibility frontier is, suppose that the public reduces consumption per capita in period $t - 1$ by an infinitesimal amount x. The budget constraint (5.3) implies that capital per capita rises by $x/(1 + n)$ in period t. Therefore, net income per capita rises by $x/(1 + n)$ times the net marginal product of capital $sb(1 + a)^{(1-s)t}K_t^{s-1} - d$. From the public's point of view, people can raise their consumption in period t by the extra $x/(1 + n)$ units of capital per capita plus the extra net income per capita by the extra capital less the extra taxes that the government takes. If the tax rate on this extra net income in period t is T_t, then sacrificing x units of consumption per capita in period $t - 1$ can

---

14. This assumption is, of course, the simplest possible one.

yield

$$x \; \frac{\left[1 + (1 - T_t)(sb(1 + a)^{(1-s)t} K_t^{s-1} - d\right]}{1 + n} \tag{5.4}$$

of consumption per capita in period t.

In equilibrium, the marginal rate of substitution, which is given by the expression (5.2), must equal the marginal private rate of transformation, which equals the negative of (5.4). Consequently,

$$(1 + r)(C_t/C_{t-1})^e = \frac{1 + (1 - T_t)(sb(1 + a)^{(1-s)t} K_t^{s-1} - d)}{1 + n} \tag{5.5}$$

We can rewrite equations (5.3) and (5.5) more compactly as

$$(c_t/c_{t-1})^e = \frac{1 + (1 - T_t)(sbk_t^{s-1} - d)}{1 + n} \tag{5.6}$$

and

$$c_t = (1-g_t)bk_t^a - (1+n)(1+a)k_{t+1} - (1-d)k_t \quad t = 2,3,\ldots \tag{5.7}$$

where

$$c_t = (1 + a)^{-t} C_t$$

$$k_t = (1 + a)^{-t} K_t$$

and

$$g_t = (1 + a)^{-t} G_t/bk_t^s$$

Appendix A establishes the following proposition: there is one, and only one, trajectory for detrended consumption c_t and the detrended capital stock k_t that simultaneously satisfies equations (5.6) and (5.7) and a transversality condition, which essentially requires c_t and k_t to converge to constants. It is also shown there that the more rapidly T_t rises, the more consumption is shifted toward the present, the more detrended capital stock is lowered, and the more social costs are incurred. Therefore, the higher the inflation rate and the longer it is allowed to affect the marginal tax rate on the net income from capital, the higher current consumption is, the lower the detrended capital stock and detrended consumption are in the long run, and the greater the social cost is.

5. Simulating the Effects of a Rising Marginal Tax Rate

In this section, I parameterize the model (5.6) and (5.7) so that it has at least some resemblance to the U.S. economy. I then simulate it for several paths that T_t might take over the next decade.

In Appendix B, I argue that the following are reasonable parameter values:

$$d = .06$$

$$g = .09$$

$$n = .015 \qquad\qquad (5.8)$$

$$s = .42$$

I also attempt to assign reasonable values to T_t, the marginal tax rate on the income from capital, for the Great Inflation years 1972-1980. These values are plotted in Figure 5.3.

It is difficult to predict just exactly what will happen to T_t in the future, but the four scenarios in Figure 5.3 seem to span the range of possibilities. All scenarios assume that the price level rises 10 percent each year between 1980 and 1990.[15] Scenarios A, B, and C assume that the federal government indexes its tax code in 1980, 1985, and 1990, respectively.[16] Between 1980 and that date, T_t rises .0066 each year.[17] Scenario D assumes that the federal government does not index the tax code until 1990, but that it does lower statuatory tax rates more rapidly than previous experience would suggest. To be specific, it assumes that T_t rises only .0033 per year between 1980 and 1990.[18]

Rather than assigning a single value to a, the rate of Harrod-neutral growth, and e and r, the preference parameters, I have simulated the

---

15. I make this assumption to show what a higher inflation rate does to the U.S. economy. I still hope that the inflation rate will really be much lower than this. The current record-breaking interest rates on bonds, however, suggest that participants in the bond markets are no longer hopeful.

16. In simulations not reported in this paper, I found that the economy is driven into the ground (k_t approaches zero) if the federal government never indexes its tax code. I therefore assume that indexing eventually occurs.

17. In Section 3, I showed that the marginal federal income tax rate tends to rise .0156 each year when the inflation rate is 10 percent per year. I show in the appendix that each percentage point rise in the marginal federal income tax rate increases T by .4219 percentage points. Therefore, T_t rises by .0066 (.4219 × .0156) each year.

18. Another way to interpret scenario D is that the inflation rate is lower than 10 percent per year.

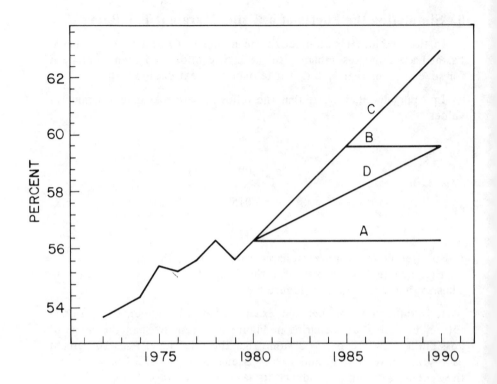

Figure 5.3
Four Scenarios for the Marginal Tax Rate on Income from Capital

model (5.6) and (5.7) for the following twelve combinations of a, e, and r:

$$a = .0075, \quad e = 0.5, \quad r = .02$$
$$a = .0075, \quad e = 0.5, \quad r = .03$$
$$a = .0075, \quad e = 1.5, \quad r = .02$$
$$a = .0075, \quad e = 1.5, \quad r = .03$$
$$a = .0075, \quad e = 2.5, \quad r = .02$$
$$a = .0075, \quad e = 2.5, \quad r = .03$$
$$a = .0125, \quad e = 0.5, \quad r = .02 \qquad (5.9)$$
$$a = .0125, \quad e = 0.5, \quad r = .03$$
$$a = .0125, \quad e = 1.5, \quad r = .02$$
$$a = .0125, \quad e = 1.5, \quad r = .03$$
$$a = .0125, \quad e = 2.5, \quad r = .02$$
$$a = .0125, \quad e = 2.5, \quad r = .03$$

I assume that the public believed dogmatically before 1972 that T_t would be .5367 in 1972 and in every subsequent year. I further assume that the public changed its beliefs at the onset of the Great Inflation. Its new beliefs were that T_t would follow one of the trajectories laid out in Figure 5.3.[19] Next, I assume that the U.S. economy would have been in steady-state equilibrium in 1972 if the public had not changed its beliefs then. Finally, I normalize k_t to be 1 in 1972. Equation (5.6), together with these assumptions, implies that

$$\frac{(1 - .5367)(.42b/1^{.58} - .06)}{1.01539(1 + a)^e(1 + r)} = 1$$

or

$$b = -4.9963 + 5.2182(1 + a)^e(1 + r) \qquad (5.10)$$

Thus,, any given values of a, e and r imply a value of b.

I have carried out forty-eight simulations, one for each scenario and each (a,e,r) combination in (5.9). Tables 5.1 through 5.4 and Figure 5.4 report some of the results of these simulations.

Table 5.1 records the percentage jump in consumption at the beginning of the simulation. The theoretical analysis in Section 4 suggested that the longer and more quickly the marginal tax rate on the income

---

19. This assumption is not very reasonable. It is hard to believe that the public correctly foresaw that there would be a Great Inflation and that it would raise T_t as much as it has. It is, however, impossible to entertain any other assumption while using the model (5.6) and (5.7). Uncertainty about T_t makes the public solve a stochastic control problem, which is too intractable to be used in this paper.

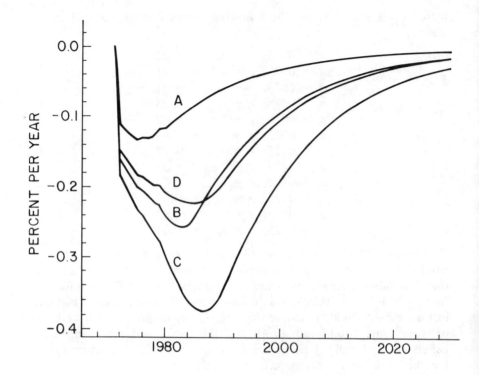

Figure 5.4
Four Possible Trajectories for the Growth Rate
of Detrended Output per Worker

TABLE 5.1

Initial Percentage Increase in Consumption

a	e	r	Scenario A	Scenario B	Scenario C	Scenario D
.0075	.5	.02	1.64	2.35	2.69	2.17
.0075	.5	.03	1.53	2.06	2.27	1.91
.0075	1.5	.02	0.92	1.41	1.68	1.30
.0075	1.5	.03	0.85	1.23	1.41	1.13
.0075	2.5	.02	0.63	0.97	1.16	0.90
.0075	2.5	.03	0.58	0.85	0.98	0.78
.0125	.5	.02	1.68	2.39	2.72	2.21
.0125	.5	.03	1.56	2.09	2.29	1.93
.0125	1.5	.02	0.90	1.34	1.56	1.24
.0125	1.5	.03	0.83	1.17	1.33	1.08
.0125	2.5	.02	0.60	0.87	1.00	0.80
.0125	2.5	.03	0.55	0.76	0.85	0.70

from capital is expected to rise, the more consumption would jump. Since moving the date of indexing from 1980 to 1985 or from 1985 to 1990 or raising the rate that T_t rises from .0033 to .0066 always increases the amount that consumption jumps, this implication of the theory holds up in these simulations. Consumption also appears to jump more when the subjective rate of time preference is lower and e is smaller.[20] The rate of Harrod-neutral growth appears to have little effect on how much consumption jumps. The jump ranges between .5 and 2.7 percent, averaging 1.4 percent.

Table 5.2 records the percentage amount that the long-run path of the capital stock drops. As suggested in the previous section, this drop increases in moving from scenario A to scenario B, from scenario B to scenario C, or from scenario D to scenario C. Thus, the drop is larger the longer and the more quickly T_t is expected to rise. Furthermore, the drop is larger the higher the subjective rate of time preference is, the larger e is, and the higher the rate of Harrod-neutral growth is. The size of the drop is between 5.9 and 29.0 percent, averaging 16.2 percent.

Table 5.3 records the percentage amount that the long-run path of consumption falls. The conclusions to be drawn from this table are exactly analogous to those drawn for the long-run path of the capital stock from Table 5.2. This is true because in long-run equilibrium, consumption is a function of only the capital stock. The fall in consumption ranges between 1.3 and 9.0 percent, averaging 4.3 percent.

Each simulation produced a trajectory for the growth rate of detrended output. Figure 5.4 plots the trajectories for scenarios A, B, C, and D when $a = .0075$, $e = 1.5$, and $r = .03$. These four trajectories are similar to the other forty-four that I do not report here. In the figure each division on the abscissa represents 4 years.

In scenario A, the growth rate of detrended output drops .11 percentage points in 1972, reaches a trough of $-.13$ percent in 1975, and then converges fairly smoothly toward zero, its long-run value. In scenario B, the growth rate drops .16 percentage points in 1972, reaches a trough of $-.26$ percent of 1983, and then converges smoothly toward zero. In scenario C, the growth rate drops .18 percentage points in 1972, falls precipitously toward its trough of $-.37$ percent in 1987, and then converges rapidly toward zero. Finally, in scenario D, the growth rate drops $-.15$ percentage points in 1972, reaches its trough of $-.22$ in

---

20. The parameter e affects the substitutability of consumption between different years. The smaller e is, the more substitutability there is.

TABLE 5.2

Percentage Reduction in the Steady-State Capital Stock

a	e	r	Scenario A	Scenario B	Scenario C	Scenario D
.0075	.5	.02	5.92	14.15	23.36	14.15
.0075	.5	.03	6.46	15.42	25.40	15.42
.0075	1.5	.02	6.35	15.15	24.97	15.15
.0075	1.5	.03	6.79	16.18	26.63	16.18
.0075	2.5	.02	6.70	15.96	26.28	15.96
.0075	2.5	.03	7.07	16.82	27.65	16.82
.0125	.5	.02	6.07	14.51	23.94	14.51
.0125	.5	.03	6.58	15.69	25.83	15.69
.0125	1.5	.02	6.70	15.96	26.27	15.96
.0125	1.5	.03	7.07	16.82	27.64	16.82
.0125	2.5	.02	7.15	17.02	27.96	17.02
.0125	2.5	.03	7.44	17.67	29.00	17.67

TABLE 5.3

Percentage Reduction in the Steady-State Level of Consumption

a	e	r	Scenario A	Scenario B	Scenario C	Scenario D
.0075	.5	.02	1.28	3.16	5.37	3.16
.0075	.5	.03	1.63	3.97	6.68	3.97
.0075	1.5	.02	1.55	3.79	6.40	3.79
.0075	1.5	.03	1.84	4.47	7.50	4.47
.0075	2.5	.02	1.78	4.33	7.26	4.33
.0075	2.5	.03	2.03	4.91	8.19	4.91
.0125	.5	.02	1.28	3.16	5.38	3.16
.0125	.5	.03	1.62	3.95	6.66	3.95
.0125	1.5	.02	1.70	4.14	6.96	4.14
.0125	1.5	.03	1.96	4.74	7.93	4.74
.0125	2.5	.02	2.02	4.89	8.16	4.89
.0125	2.5	.03	2.22	5.36	8.92	5.36

1985, and then converges smoothly toward zero. I conclude that the growth rate is lower the longer the tax code remains unindexed, the fewer statutory tax changes offset the effects of inflation, and the higher the inflation rate. It is important to note that inflation has already reduced the growth rate by a substantial amount (scenario A) and that failure to index the tax code this year will put a further drag on growth.[21]

Inflation leads to a rising marginal federal income tax rate, which imposes social costs on the public. In other words, the public would have been willing in 1972 to have paid something to have avoided the inflation that occurred after that date. The largest amount that the public would have been willing to pay is a measure of the social cost of these effects. Table 5.4 reports estimates of the social costs of inflation for each (a,e,r) combination and for each scenario. Appendix C derives the formula used for these calculations. The social costs are expressed as a percent of total consumption in 1972.

Clearly, the social costs noted in Table 5.4 are enormous. They rise a great deal as the date of indexing moves from 1980 to 1985 or from 1985 to 1990 and also as ΔT_t increases from .0033 to .0066. Furthermore, they become larger as the subjective rate of time preference decreases and as e becomes smaller. I conclude that the Great Inflation has created large social costs, social costs large enough to give the public ample reason to cry out against inflation.

For purposes of comparison, I have calculated the social costs of several possible "recessions" that might have been required during the 1972-1980 period in order to have prevented the Great Inflation. These "recessions" reduce national income by an equal percentage amount each year between 1972 and 1980, but they have no effect on the steady-state path of the capital stock or on the productivity of the economy after 1980. I find that a 1.5 percent reduction in national income has a social cost of about 20 percent of consumption in 1972, that a 9-percent reduction has a social cost of 66 percent of consumption in 1972; and that it takes an 18-percent reduction in national income to have a social cost as high as 240 percent of consumption in 1972.[22]

---

21. It is important to note again that these paths for the growth rate assume that the public predicted the rapid rise in T_t as early as 1972. In reality, the public probably came to this view only gradually between 1972 and 1980. If so, the fall in the growth rate that Figure 5.2 shows occurring in 1972 would probably have been distributed over the years 1972-1980. Furthermore, the growth rate will probably be lower in the years after 1980 than the figure suggests.

22. These social costs are not very sensitive to my assumptions about a, e, and r.

TABLE 5.4

Compensation for Inflation as a Percent of Consumption in 1972

a	e	r	Scenario A	Scenario B	Scenario C	Scenario D
.0075	.5	.02	44.6	109.0	182.2	107.3
.0075	.5	.03	30.5	69.5	113.5	68.4
.0075	1.5	.02	28.9	68.4	112.1	66.8
.0075	1.5	.03	20.7	47.2	74.9	45.7
.0075	2.5	.02	19.8	46.1	74.2	44.7
.0075	2.5	.03	14.7	33.0	51.6	31.6
.0125	.5	.02	57.8	143.1	240.1	138.0
.0125	.5	.03	36.8	84.2	137.8	83.2
.0125	1.5	.02	28.8	67.3	108.9	65.5
.0125	1.5	.03	20.6	46.6	73.4	45.0
.0125	2.5	.02	16.9	38.1	59.7	36.7
.0125	2.5	.03	12.9	28.2	42.9	27.0

Therefore, the public would almost surely have preferred a 1.5-percent recession over the period 1972-1980 to the inflation that has actually taken place. The public may well have preferred a 5-percent recession to the inflation. It is even conceivable that they would have preferred an incredibly deep, 18-percent recession to the inflation. If so, the inflation since 1972 may rival the Great Depression as a social problem, and thus it may not be inappropriate to use my label "the Great Inflation."

Of course, we should keep in mind that these latter results came from a highly simplified, and perhaps unrealistic, model of the U.S. economy. Whether they will hold up in richer models is an open question that future work must resolve.

6. Conclusions

Inflation has harmful effects only if it is not perfectly anticipated or if at least one economic agent in the economy fails to adjust completely. I have presented evidence that the most important agent in the U.S. economy, the federal government, does not adjust completely to inflation. A rapid inflation spells a rapidly rising marginal tax rate on personal income, which in turn spells a rapidly escalating marginal tax rate on the income from capital.

I have constructed a model of the U.S. economy and have simulated it in order to assess the effects of the Great Inflation. The results of these simulations strongly suggest that the growth rate of the economy has been depressed on the order of .1 to .4 percentage points and that this slower growth has led to an enormous social cost. The social cost is probably in excess of 50 percent of consumption in 1972, thus justifying my labeling the period since 1972 the Great Inflation.

Appendix A

For the public to be maximizing its utility, the trajectories of detrended consumption and the detrended stock of capital must obey equations (5.6) and (5.7). The capital stock is predetermined in year 1, the first year of the program. Once the public selects c_1, the entire trajectories of c_t and k_t are determined.

Figure 5A.1 illustrates how the public selects c_1 when T_t and g_t are the constants T^* and g. The vertical curve labeled $c_t = c_{t-1}$ is obtained by setting $c_t = c_{t-1}$ in equation (5.6):

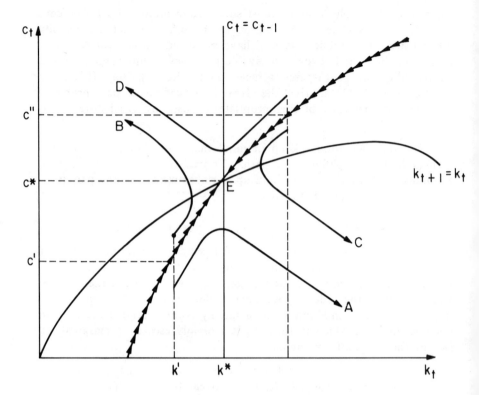

Figure 5A.1
The Optimal Path of Accumulation

$$\frac{1 + (1 - T^*)(sbk_t^{s-1} - d)}{(1 + n)(1 + a)^e(1 + r)} = 1$$

or

$$k_t = k^* \tag{5A.1}$$

where

$$k^* = \left[\frac{sb(1 - T^*)}{(1 + n)(1 + a)^e(1 + r) + d(1 - T^*) - 1}\right]^{\frac{1}{1-s}} \tag{5A.2}$$

Along it c_t is constant; to its left, c_t is rising; and to its right, c_t is falling.[23] The curve labeled $k_{t+1} = k_t$ is obtained by setting $k_{t+1} = k_t$ in equation (5.7):

$$(1 + n)(1 + a)k_t = (1 - d)k_t + (1 - g)bk_t^s - c_t$$

or

$$c_t = (1 - g)bk_t^s - [(1 + n)(1 + a) + d - 1]k_t \tag{5A.3}$$

This curve passes through the origin, slopes upward near $k_t = 0$, and is concave.[24] Along it k_t stays constant; above it k_t is falling; and below it k_t is falling.[25] There is only one combination of k_t and c_t for which neither k_t nor c_t changes. This combination (k^*, c^*) is located at the point E in Figure 5A.1.

Suppose that the public starts out with $k_1 = k'$, which is less than k^*, and suppose further that the public sets c_1 at a value slightly less than c'. Figure 5A.1 shows that k_t and c_t then follow the diverging path A. If instead c_1 is set slightly higher than c', k_t and c_t follow the diverging path B. Only the setting $c_1 = c'$ results in a path that converges to point E. Similarly, if k_1 had been k'', which is larger than k^*, every setting of c_1 except c'' results in a diverging path like C or D.

---

23. The right-hand members of equation (5.6) are a decreasing function of k_t since $s < 1$. Therefore, if $k_t < k^*$, $c_t/c_{t-1} > 1$; if $k_t > k^*$, $c_t/c_{t-1} < 1$.

24. At $k_t = 0$ the right-hand member of equation (5A.3) is 0. Its derivative is $(1 - g)sbk_t^{s-1} - [(1 + n)(1 + a) + d - 1]$, which approaches infinity as k_t approaches zero. Its second derivative is $(1 - g)s(s - 1)bk_t^{s-2}$, which is negative.

25. One can rewrite equation (5.7) as

$$k_{t+1} - k_t = (1 - g)bk_t^s - [(1 - n)(1 + a) + d - 1]k_t - c_t.$$

When equation (5A.3) is satisfied, the right-hand member of the above equation is zero. When c_t is too low to satisfy equation (5A.3) for any given k_t, the right-hand member is positive. When c_t is too high to satisfy equation (5A.3) for any given k_t, the right-hand member is negative.

Only the setting c'' leads to point E. Since the transversality condition requires that k_t and c_t converge to constants, only one setting of c_1 can be optimal for any given initial k_t.

Suppose that T_t has been T^* for many years prior to year 1 and that the public dogmatically believed during that period that T_t would be T^* forever.[26] During this period k_t and c_t converged to k^* and c^*. Next, suppose that in year 1 inflation begins in earnest, that the tax code is not indexed, that the government does not adjust completely to inflation, and that T_t therefore starts to rise. The public immediately realizes what is happening. It now believes dogmatically that T_t will rise over the next h years, reaching

$$T_h = T^{**} > T^*$$

and that, in year h, the government will index its tax code so that T_t stays constant at T^{**} thereafter.

Since the world changes in year 1, the household recalculates its optimal path of accumulation. Figure 5A.2 shows the path that the public chooses. The variable c_t rises to c_1 in year 1. As T_t rises over time, the $c_t = c_{t-1}$ locus

$$k_t = \left[\frac{sb(1 - T_t)}{(1 + n)(1 + a)^e(1 + r) + d(1 - T_t) - 1} \right]^{\frac{1}{1-s}} \quad (5A.2)$$

shifts to the left.[27] Starting at this time, the economy then follows the path IJE^{**}. This path consists of a segment IJ that takes the economy to GH, the optimal accumulation path for the new steady state, in year h. Thereafter, the economy follows the segment JE^{**}. If the public chooses any level of consumption other than c', c_t and k_t follow a diverging path like A or B, and the transversality condition is violated.

This analysis suggests that inflation together with an unindexed tax system initially raises consumption (c jumps in year 1 from c^* to c'); the higher consumption then results in a lower growth rate of per capita capital and output over some period (k begins to fall);[28] and this lower

---

26. This belief must be dogmatic for the mathematical techniques used in deriving (5.6) and (5.7) to be valid.

27.

$$\frac{dk_t^{1-s}}{dT_t} = \frac{[(1 + n)(1 + a)^e(1 + r) - 1]sb}{[(1 + n)(1 + a)^e(1 + r) + d(11 - T_t) - 1]^2} < 0$$

28. The growth rate of capital per worker in year t is defined to be

$$\log\left(\frac{K_t/N_t}{K_{t-1}/N_{t-1}} \right) = \log(1 + a) + \log(k_t/k_{t-1})$$

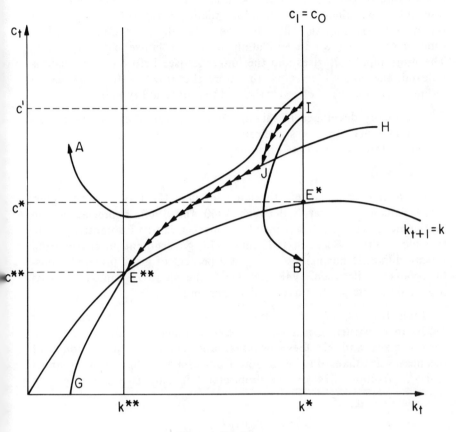

Figure 5A.2
The Optimal Accumulation Path
When the Marginal Tax Rate Is Rising

growth rate of per capita output eventually forces detrended consumption to be lower than it was when the inflation began ($c^{**} < c^*$). Even though consumption initially rises and only falls after some period of time, it can be shown that inflation makes the household worse off.[29] The more rapidly T_t rises and the longer it rises before the tax code is indexed, the larger $c' - c^*$ is, the more the growth rate of per capita output falls, the larger $c^* - c^{**}$ is, and the more utility falls.

The theory developed in this appendix suggests that a rising marginal tax rate may have a significant effect on per capita consumption, capital, and output and thus on utility.

Appendix B

Between 1948 and 1967, the labor input of the U.S. economy grew 1.539 percent per year.[30] Between 1960 and 1969, depreciation and replacement averaged 6 percent of the market value of domestic private tangible wealth.[31] Between 1972 and 1978, government purchases from private domestic businesses averaged 9 percent of gross private domestic product.[32] Between 1948 and 1967, the share of capital in gross private domestic product averaged 42 percent.[33]

Table B.1 provides an estimate of the net income from capital for 1972. In constructing this table, I have assumed that all property and wealth taxes and all fees, licenses, and taxes on the conduct of businesses are taxes on the income from capital. I have also assumed that the fraction .374 of net proprietors' income is a net return to

---

Output per worker is

$$(1 + a)^{(1-s)t} bN_t^{1-s} K^s / N_t = (1 + a)^t bk_t^s$$

Its growth rate in year t is defined to be

$$\log\left[\frac{(1 + a)^t bk_t^s}{(1 + a)^{t-1} bk_t^s}\right] = \log(1 + a) + s \log(k_t/k_{t-1})$$

29. This statement follows immediately from the maximum principle.

30. See Table 4 of Christensen and Jorgenson (1970).

31. See Tables 13 and 19 of Christensen and Jorgenson (1973).

32. Government purchases from private businesses equals government purchases of goods and services (1.1.21), less government product (1.7.2), less government product (1.7.12), less income produced in government enterprises (1.14.34), plus the service flow from consumer durables. I approximated the service flow from consumer durables with the purchases of consumer durables (1.1.13). The numbers in parentheses refer to tables and rows in *National Income and Product Accounts*. For example, 1.1.21 indicates Row 21 of Table 1.1.

33. See Table 6 of Christensen and Jorgenson (1970).

TABLE 5B.1

Net Income from Capital in 1972

	Item	Amount[p]
(1)	Dividends[a]	17,914
(2)	Undistributed corporate profits + IVA + CCA[b]	24,597
(3)	Federal profits tax liability[c]	36,560
(4)	State profits tax liability[d]	4,975
(5)	Proprietors' income from capital[e]	28,475
(6)	Net interest from owner-occupied housing[f]	21,500
(7)	Net interest except from owners-occupied housing[g]	25,528
(8)	Rental income from owner-occupied housing	11,500
(9)	Indirect business taxes levied on owner-occupied housing[i]	16,900
(10)	Rental income except that from owner-occupied housing[j]	17,914
(11)	Nontaxes on rents and royalties[k]	993
(12)	Indirect business taxes levied on business income except that from owner-occupied housing[l]	37,285
(13)	Estate, gift, and death taxes[m]	6,804
(14)	Total net income from capital	250,945
(15)	Net income from owner-occupied housing[n]	49,900
(16)	Net income from capital except that from owner-occupied housing[o]	201,045

a 1.13.25
b 1.13.26 + 1.13.27 + 1.13.28
c 3.2.23
d 3.4.13
e The fraction .374 of total proprietors' income (1.13.9)
f 8.3.67
g 1.13.29 − 8.3.67
h 8.3.68
i 8.3.65

j 1.13.17 − 8.3.68
k 3.4.27
l 3.2.18 + 3.4.5 + 3.4.6 + 3.4.7 + 3.4.23 + 3.4.24 + 3.4.25 + 3.4.28 + 3.4.29 + 3.4.30
m 3.2.7 + 3.4.4
n (6) + (8) + (9)
o (14) − (15)
p In billions of dollars

capital[34] and that consumers' durables produce no net income.[35]

The items in Table 5B.1 can be grouped into six categories: dividends, capital gains, interest, proprietors' income from capital, rental income from owner-occupied housing, and other rental income. Each of these six categories of income is taxed differently.

Dividends are one part of corporate profits. They are first subject to property taxes and other taxes on the conduct of business. I assume that these taxes take 21.24 percent of dividends.[36] The remaining 78.76 percent is then subject to a marginal state profits tax of 5.40 percent.[37] Next, the remaining 74.51 percent is subject to a 48 percent marginal federal profits tax rate between 1972 and 1978 and to a 46 percent rate thereafter. State governments then impose income taxes on dividends, followed by the federal government. I assume that if the marginal federal income tax rate is z, the combination of state and federal income taxes is levied at the rate of $1.1z$.[38] Finally, estate, gift, and death taxes are levied on what remains at the rate of .0545.[39] Therefore, the marginal tax rate on dividends is

$$.6334 + .4032z, \quad 1972\text{-}1978$$

$$.6194 + .4187z, \quad 1979\text{-} \tag{5B.1}$$

Capital gains, another part of corporate profits, are subject to the same taxes as dividends up to the point where income taxes are paid. I assume that a dollar of retained earnings results in a dollar of capital

34. This figure is the ratio of gross private domestic outlays for the services of noncorporate business capital as reported in Table 8 of Christensen and Jorgenson (1973), less capital consumption allowances (6.15.2) to net proprietors' income (1.13.9).

35. This assumption is approximately true. See Tables 8 and 13 Christensen and Jorgenson (1973) and Table 1.13 of the *National Income and Product Accounts*.

36. This figure is the ratio of item (12) to item (16), less items (6) and (7). The implicit assumptions in this calculation are that all the taxes in item (12) are proportional to the net income of business capital and that they are paid by stockholders, proprietors, and the owners of rental property.

37. This figure is the ratio of item (4) to the sum of items (1), (2), (3), and (4).

38. In 1972, state income taxes (3.4.3) were 17.00 percent of federal income taxes (3.2.3). Since state income taxes are often less progressive than the federal income tax forms, $1.17z$ is probably an upper bound to the marginal income tax rate, while z is certainly a lower bound. The figure $1.1z$ is a compromise between these two extremes.

39. This figure is the ratio of item (13) to item (14), less items (3), (4), (9), (11), and (12), less income taxes on the income from capital. Income taxes on the income from capital are 24.5 percent of total income taxes (3.2.3 + 3.4.3). The factor .245 is the average fraction of income taxes attributed by Christensen and Jorgenson (1973, p. 336), to the income from capital.

gains, that the realization of capital gains is deferred long enough that only the fraction .4 of retained earnings is ever subject to income taxation, and that the tax code exempts 50 percent of capital gains from taxation between 1972 and 1978 and 60 percent thereafter.[40] I further assume that estate, gift, and death taxes capture 5.45 percent of the remainder. These assumptions imply that the marginal tax rate on capital gains is

$$.6334 + .0763z, \quad 1972\text{-}1978$$

$$.6194 + .0670z, \quad 1979\text{-} \tag{5B.2}$$

Interest is not subject to property taxes and other taxes on business; nor is it subject to the corporate profits tax. It is, however, subject to income taxation at the rate $1.1z$ and then to estate, gift, and death taxes at the rate of 5.45 percent. Consequently, the marginal tax rate on interest is

$$.0545 + 1.040z \tag{5B.3}$$

The income from proprietors' capital is subject to property taxes at the rate of 21.24 percent. The remaining 78.76 percent is then subject to income taxation at the rate $1.1z$. What is finally left after income taxation is subject to estate, gift, and death taxes at the rate of 5.45 percent. The marginal tax rate on the income from proprietors' capital is therefore

$$.2549 + .8196z \tag{5B.4}$$

The rental income from owner-occupied housing is subject to property taxes at the rate of 59.51 percent.[41] These taxes, however, are deductions from the income tax, which is levied at the rate $1.1z$. What is then left over is subject to estate, gift, and death taxes at the rate of 5.45 percent. Consequently, the marginal tax rate on the income from owner-occupied housing is

$$.6170 - .6193z \tag{5B.5}$$

Other rental income is subject to property and other business taxes at the rate of 21.24 percent. In addition, nontaxes are imposed on other rental income at the rate of 5.54 percent.[42] After paying these taxes, the owners of rental property pay income taxes. Finally, they

---

40. Inflation may raise the fraction of capital gains that are ever subject to income tax because it creates nominal capital gains. I am ignoring this effect.

41. This figure is the ratio of item (9) to item (8), plus item (9).

42. This figure is the ratio of item (11) to the sum of items (10) and (11).

pay estate, gift, and death taxes at the rate of 5.45 percent. Altogether, their marginal tax rate is

$$.3073 + .7619z \tag{5B.6}$$

In 1972, dividends, capital gains, interest, the income from proprietors' capital, the rental income from owner-occupied housing, and other rental income accounted for 18.62, 25.57, 19.26, 14.97, 11.63, and 9.94 percent of total net income from capital, respectively.[43] Weighting the marginal tax rates by these fractions then yields

$$T_t = .4370 + .4214z, \quad 1972\text{-}1978$$

$$T_t = .4308 + .4219z, \quad 1979\text{-} \tag{5B.7}$$

I obtained the tax rates for 1972-1979 plotted in Figure 5.4 by replacing z with the marginal federal income tax rate on ordinary income that Ranson et al. (1979) have calculated. I estimated in Section 3 that z rises 1.56 percentage points per year when the inflation rate is 10 percent per year. Since the GNP deflator will rise approximately 10 percent between 1979 and 1980, T_t will be approximately .0066 (= .4219 × .0156) higher in 1980 than in 1979.

Appendix C

One utility function that yields the marginal rate of substitution (5.2) is

$$\sum_{t=1}^{\infty} \left[\frac{1}{1+r} \right]^t \left[\frac{C_t^{1-e} - 1}{1 - e} \right] \quad r,e > 0 \tag{5C.1}$$

(One can prove this assertion by implicitly differencing C_t with respect to C_{t-1} in equation (5C.1).) I assume that this is the utility function that the public uses to value alternative trajectories for per-capita consumption.

Suppose that the economy starts at time 1 in a long-run equilibrium with $k_1 = 1$ and that the economy stays in this equilibrium. Then detrended consumption is[44]

---

43. I allocated items (6) and (7) to interest; items (8) and (9) to rental income from owner-occupied housing; items (10) and (11) to other rental income; items (3) and (4) to dividends and capital gains in proportion to their sizes; item (12) to dividends, capital gains, the income from proprietors' capital, and other rental income in proportion to their sizes; and item (13) to all categories of income in proportion to their sizes.

44. One can obtain this equation by substituting $k_{t+1} = k_t = 1$ into equation (5B.3). Remember that k_t is normalized to be 1 in 1972 and that it is assumed that the

$$c_0 = 1 + (1 - g)b - d - (1 + n)(1 + a)$$

in every time period t. Therefore, utility is given by

$$U_0 = \frac{1}{1-e} \left\{ \sum_{t=1}^{\infty} \left[\frac{(1+a)^{1-e}}{1+r} \right]^t (c_0^{1-e} - 1) \right\}$$

$$= \frac{1}{1-e} \left\{ \frac{[(1+a)c_0]^{1-e}}{1+r-(1+a)^{1-e}} - \frac{1}{r} \right\}$$

or

$$\frac{1}{1-e} \frac{[(1+a)c_0]^{1-e}}{1+r-(1+a)^{1-e}} = U_0 + \frac{1}{1-e}\frac{1}{r} \qquad (5C.2)$$

When scenario i is followed, c_t follows a trajectory that yields a utility defined as U_i. Let m satisfy

$$\frac{1}{1-e} \left\{ \frac{[(1+a)c_0 \exp(-m)]^{1-e}}{1+r-(1+a)^{1-e}} - \frac{1}{r} \right\} = U_i$$

or

$$\frac{1}{1-e} \frac{[(1+a)c_0]^{1-e}\exp[-(1-e)m]}{1+r-(1+a)^{1-e}} = U_i + \frac{1}{1-e}\frac{1}{r} \qquad (5C.3)$$

Dividing equation (5C.2) by (5C.3) then yields

$$\exp[(1-e)m] = \frac{U_0 + \dfrac{1}{1-e}\dfrac{1}{r}}{U_i + \dfrac{1}{1-e}\dfrac{1}{r}}$$

or

$$m = \frac{1}{1-e} \log \left[\frac{U_0 + \dfrac{1}{1-e}\dfrac{1}{r}}{U_i + \dfrac{1}{1-e}\dfrac{1}{r}} \right]$$

The present value of the fraction m of consumption in 1972 and in every future year is then[45]

---

economy would have been in steady-state equilibrium in that year, had T_t not began to rise.

45. In any steady-state equilibrium, the discount factor is the reciprocal of $(1+n)(1+a)$; discounting the fraction m of consumption in 1972 and every future year yields the term in the first set of brackets in equation (5C.4) times m.

164   Paul Evans

$$X_i = \left[\frac{1+r}{1+r(1+a)^{1-e}}\right]\left[\frac{1}{1-e}\right]\log\left[\frac{U_0+\dfrac{1}{1-e}\dfrac{1}{r}}{U_i+\dfrac{1}{1-e}\dfrac{1}{r}}\right] \quad (5C.4)$$

The quantity X_i is the largest amount that the public would be willing to pay to replace scenario i with a constant detrended consumption c_0.

References

Business Statistics. 1977. Bureau of Economic Analysis. Washington, D.C.: Government Printing Office.

Cass, D. 1965. "Optimal Growth in an Aggregate Model of Capital Accumulation." *Review of Economic Studies* 32 (July), pp. 233-243.

Christensen, L. R., and D. W. Jorgenson. 1970. "U.S. Real Product and Real Factor Input, 1929-1967." *Review of Income and Wealth*, Series 16, No. 1 (March), pp. 19-50.

Christensen, L. R., and D. W. Jorgenson. 1973. "U.S. Income Saving and Wealth, 1929-1969." *The Review of Income and Wealth*, Series 19, No. 4 (December), pp. 329-362.

Fisher, S., and F. Modigliani. 1978. "Towards an Understanding of the Real Effects and Costs of Inflation." *Weltwirtschaftliches Archiv* 114, pp. 810-833.

National Income and Product Accounts of the United States, 1929-74. Bureau of Economic Analysis. Washington, D.C.: Government Printing Office.

Public Opinion. 1978. Washington, D.C.: American Enterprise Institute, May/June.

Ranson, R. D., A. B. Laffer, and M. E. Weinburg. 1979. "The 'Prototype Wedge Model': A Tool for Supply-Side Economics." Boston: H. C. Wainwright and Company.

Survey of Current Business. 1977-1979. Bureau of Economic Analysis. Washington, D.C.: Government Printing Office.

Takayama, A. 1974. *Mathematical Economics.* Hinsdale, Ill.: Dryden

Press.

Yaari, M. 1964. "On the Consumer's Lifetime Allocation Process." *International Economic Review* 5 (September), pp. 304-317.

6

Some Perspectives on Controlling U.S. Inflation

Michael Bazdarich

*Claremont Economic Institute**

1. Introduction

No one reading this paper needs to be convinced or reminded that inflation is one of the most — or the most — serious problem plaguing the American economy. Other papers in this volume have pointed out that inflation rates are highly variable and unpredictable, and that statistical measures of inflation typically involve sizable measurement errors. While these remarks are undeniably true, it is equally true that the last twenty-odd years of U.S. experience have involved systematic, predictable, and sizable increases in prices as well. Otherwise, inflation would not be the center of national concern that it is.

What is more, inflation can be controlled only to the extent that it is systematic and attributable to identifiable causes, which in turn are subject to the purview and control of economic policymakers. This paper will analyze the causes of systematic inflation in the United States over the last twenty years, and thereby offer some insights on probable

* This work was done while the author was at the Federal Reserve Bank of San Francisco.

fruitful methods of controlling inflation.

A central theme of the analysis is that inflation can continue if and only if the money supply is increasing as well. It follows, therefore, that a factor can be certified as a root cause of continuing inflation only if it can be identified as a "cause" of money supply growth. This observation permits identification of the underlying causes of inflation, and at the same time avoids possibly spurious findings of causality that might be obtained by simply directly correlating a "causal" variable with the inflation rate. That is, as will be seen later, under any consistent theory of inflation, virtually all nominal (i.e., money - or dollar-denominated) variables will increase together. Most studies have attempted to identify causes of inflation by identifying correlation between inflation rates and various "causal factors." Yet because any two or more nominal variables will inevitably be increasing together in any significant inflation, identifying such correlation need not rule out the possibility that yet another variable is actually causing all the considered variables to increase in the first place.

For example, consider wages and prices. Again, *any* significant inflation will see increases in wages as well as prices. Therefore, the mere existence of a statistical relation between wages and prices cannot preclude the possibility that, say, the money supply, or perhaps oil prices, caused both wages and prices to increase and thus was the true cause of inflation. Even if prices systematically increased after wages, this could merely reflect the fact that wages responded more quickly than prices to the underlying cause of inflation.

We avoid such pratfalls if we look at the causes of money supply growth. Economic theory specifies, and experience confirms, that general inflation cannot arise or continue without accompanying increases in the money supply. If money wages or any other money price were held fixed while other nominal variables (including the money supply) were allowed to increase, inflation would proceed much the same as it has. However, if the money supply were held fixed and other variables were allowed to fluctuate freely, any resulting inflation would be quite different (would likely involve widespread increasing unemployment) and would in any case be much more short-lived than it has been. Thus, by identifying underlying causes of money supply growth, which is crucial to the continuation of inflation, we can obtain a much more reliable test of the causes of inflation.

The statistical technique used to identify causation in this study is the Granger causality test. Though it is itself merely a sophisticated method of identifying correlation between two variables, it nevertheless avoids much of the spurious types of correlation that can arise between variables with similar (upward) trends.

Section 2 describes some of the economic theory of inflation and discusses in further detail the assertions made above. Section 3 briefly explains the Granger causality technique, and Section 4 discusses results of Granger causality tests designed to identify causes of inflation by identifying causes of money supply growth. Section 5 then considers the explanatory power of the money supply and other factors for inflation in the 1971-1975 and 1978-1980 periods. Section 6 concludes the paper by returning to the issue of the controllability of inflation.

2. Inflation, the Money Supply, and Cost-Push

It is common for a noneconomist to describe as "inflation" any increase in any price or cost whatsoever, regardless of the circumstances. An economist, however, splits price increases into relative price increases and absolute price increases.

Relative price increases are typified by increases in the price of a single commodity, or a group of commodities, vis-a-vis the prices of other commodities. These usually are the result of occurrences in the "real" economy, e.g., crop failures, impositions of taxes, and supply disruptions. Absolute price increases concern roughly equal or similar-in-magnitude increases in virtually all money prices, with little accompanying change in underlying economic conditions; it is these that economists identify as inflation. In theory, these increases can persist only if they are accompanied by an increase in the money supply.

To understand this dichotomy, consider an economy in equilibrium, and suppose the cash amount of money (cash, deposits, etc.) were doubled. Suppose all money prices then doubled. Then relative prices would be unchanged. For example, two gallons of milk cost as much as one pound of beef when milk costs $1 per gallon and beef cost $2 per pound, and also when they cost $2 per gallon and $4 per pound. Therefore, the trading conditions among goods would be unchanged.

Also, since cash and deposit balances and all prices would have doubled together, the purchasing power of the stock of cash and deposit balances would be unchanged. Finally, even though the purchasing power or real value of existing credits of creditors would be smaller, these losses would be exactly matched by reductions in the real value of debts by corresponding debtors, and so on average the real buying power of the economy would remain unchanged.

Therefore, if the economy were in equilibrium before these changes, it would still be in equilibrium after these changes. In other words, a doubling of the money supply would result in a pure inflation, a doubling of all equilibrium absolute prices, with no change in relative prices.

On the other hand, let wages double and let all other prices double as well, but hold the supply of money fixed. As before, real trading conditions among goods would be unchanged. However, now the real purchasing power of the cash and deposits in the economy would be lower because the cash amount has not changed while prices are higher.

Therefore, there would not be enough money — alternatively, enough financial wealth — available to finance the previous real flow of goods at the higher money (absolute) prices, so the economy could not then be in equilibrium. Something would have to change: some prices and wages would have to fall, and employment would shift among industries, depending of course on what disturbance caused wages to rise in the first place. Much the same analysis would hold for other types of "inflationary" disturbances, whether they be increases in oil prices or food prices, or changes in the government deficit.

The point is that either the disturbance would be temporary and short-lived, or else it would result primarily in relative price changes and movements of resources across industries, but not in the absolute-price inflation discussed earlier. The latter requires an increase in the money supply in order for previous equilibrium flows of goods and services to be financed at generally higher money prices.

These conclusions have been stressed in the economics literature for over 200 years, and the incidence of increasing money supplies preceding or accompanying persistent inflation has been documented for almost that long.[1] Of course, in reality changes in real (nonmonetary)

---

1. The idea that an increase in the money supply should lead to an equiproportional change in all money prices, but not to any change in real conditions, goes back at least to the writings of David Hume, in the late eighteenth century, and it is likely an important factor in the way economists have come to define inflation as an absolute price increase. For a classic modern exposition of this point, and its corollaries, see Patinkin (1963). Also, Friedman (1956) presents some early econometric work

factors are always occurring alongside increases in the money supply, so that not all prices rise by equal proportion. Also, growth in the economy increases the demand for money as well, so that prices do not typically increase as rapidly as the money supply does. Still, it is remarkable how closely increases in prices on average correspond to rates suggested by the rate of increase in money, allowing for economic growth.

This coincidence does not, however, imply that increases in the money supply are the ultimate or first cause of inflation. Verifying this entails identifying why the money supply grows in the first place: why monetary authorities allow the money supply to grow excessively even though theory and experience suggest this will cause inflation. Nevertheless, as asserted in the first section, the necessary coincidence of inflation and money supply growth allows us to identify the underlying causes of inflation by identifying the causes of money supply growth. Whereas finding systematic relations between some "inflationary" factor and prices would not rule out the possibility that both these variables are increasing in response to the money supply or some other third factor, finding systematic effects from such a variable to the money supply would identify the former as a systematic root cause of inflation.

Once again, many factors, such as wage increases or oil or food price increases, commonly discused as causes of inflation should more properly be described as causes of relative price changes, of movements of productive factors across industries, and of temporary unemployment in affected industries when workers or capital are slow to respond to these economic signals. Avoidance of this unemployment and of this disruption of established commerce — painful albeit temporary — is then usually cited as the reason why the money supply would increase in response to wage or price increases, thereby allowing movements in absolute prices as well as in relative prices.

Because of political pressures, monetary authorities might plausibly "accommodate," say, oil price increases in order to avoid these disruptions. When demand is stimulated in such a way, previous flows of goods and services can be maintained at the higher price levels. The employment disruptions are avoided at the cost of inflation, an inflation that could get worse if the "offending" parties demand still higher price

---

documenting the statistical link between money and prices in a variety of economic settings. Subsequent such work includes Meiselman (1970) and a host of other published articles.

or wage increases next time around.

With similar scenarios of "monetary accommodation," we can make any inflation theory economically self-consistent by citing its particular factor as a cause of money supply growth. This suggests that such theories can and should be tested directly by determining whether their respective causal factors can explain money supply growth in various periods. Such tests are discussed in Section 4 for a wide range of wage-push, cost-push, and government-spending indicators commonly cited as causes of inflation.

3. The Granger Causality Technique

Granger causality tests are a type of regression analysis designed to avoid identifying as causality some kinds of correlations that can exist between two or more variables. The technique was first formalized by C. W. J. Granger and developed and popularized by Christopher Sims.

To understand the technique and its importance, consider first two variables x and y, which move together as in Figure 6.1 or Figure 6.2. With behavior as shown in Figure 6.1, x and y would clearly be highly correlated contemporaneously, and regressing y on x, or vice versa, would yield very significant results. With behavior as in Figure 6.2, x and y would again be highly correlated, although at some lag, and a regression of y on lagged x, or of x on lagged y, would also yield significant results. However, in Figure 6.1 the variables x and y are moving in lockstep together, and it is impossible to tell from a simple regression or correlation which is causing which, or if both are caused by some third factor. Similarly, even for the behavior shown in Figure 6.2, a simple regression will not reveal whether lagged x causes y or lagged y causes x, or neither.

Furthermore, despite the high correlation shown in both figures, it's not clear that x is useful in predicting or explaining y (or vice versa) in either case. This is because in both cases the variable y (x) can be predicted very well from its own past behavior or trend alone. Both x and y may merely exhibit common trend, with the past trend in y better able to explain subsequent movements in y itself than movements in x could. This would be the case for two variables like population and the price level, which increase over time together but have no true connection otherwise, or for two variables that are both caused by a third variable, and so exhibit related trend, but do not necessarily have any relation other than common trend. Thus, not only does

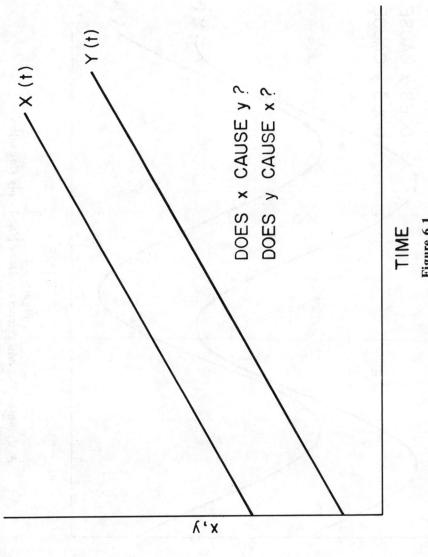

TIME

Figure 6.1
Parallel Growth Does Not Imply Causality

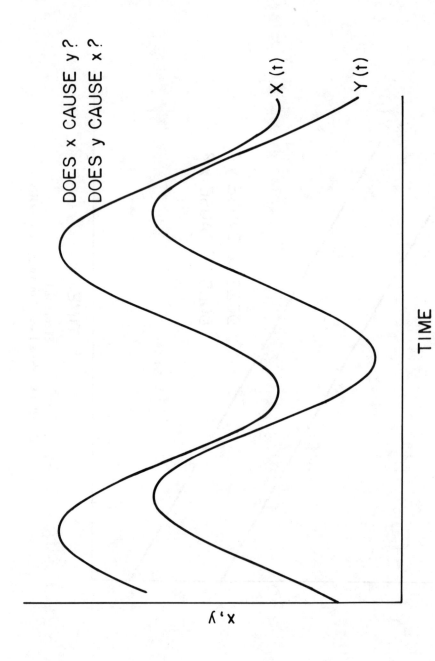

Figure 6.2

A Common Periodic Structure Does Not Imply Causality

correlation not imply causality, but correlation need not even imply a true correlation between two variables.

The Granger technique avoids identifying these types of correlation as causality by working with equations of form

$$P_T \quad = \quad \sum_{j=1}^{8} B_j P_{T-j} \quad + \quad \sum_{j=1}^{8} C_j M_{T-j} \quad + \quad E_T \quad (1)$$

| Current Inflation | is a function of.... | Lagged Inflation, | Lagged Money Growth, | & | Random Factors. |

This form includes lagged values of the dependent variable (in this case P_T) in the equation to explain subsequent movements of the dependent variable from its own past movements (i.e., from its own trend). Any significant effects of the other explanatory variables in this equation, then, would show that the explanatory variable can account for changes in the trend of the dependent variable. This is how Granger defined statistical causality in his original work: the ability of a variable, say x, to predict movements in another variable, say y, even over and above the predictive power of past y itself.

In the case of the money supply causing inflation, equation (1) as schematized in Figure 6.3 suggests that money supply growth causes, or "fuels," inflation. Once money supply growth ceases or changes, the momentum of past inflation will keep inflation continuing at its own trend rate temporarily, because of expectations and sluggish response, just as an engine can temporarily continue to turn after its fuel has been cut off. But money supply growth is providing the impulse that eventually determines the rate of inflation.

Though (1) refers specifically to money supply growth "causing" inflation, its basic form can be generalized to "causal" relationships between any two (or more variables). Thus, for an equation explaining money supply growth in terms of past money supply growth and movements in, say, wages, the idea would be that monetary authorities react to wages, with the lagged money growth variables implying that the process continues for a short period of time even after wage changes cease or change course.

Thus, an equation form similar to that in (1) may show no effects of x on y, or vice versa, for behavior as in Figure 6.1 or 6.2, since the

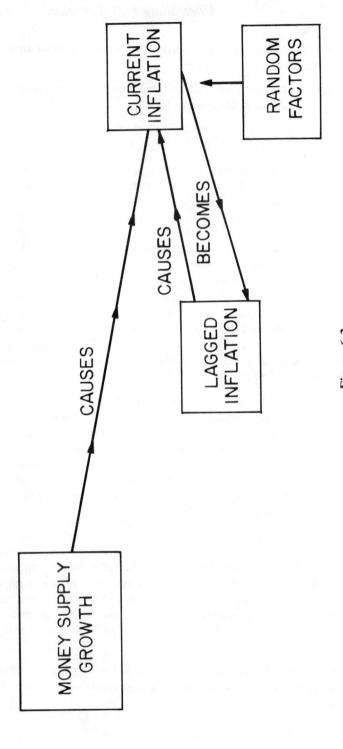

Figure 6.3
Schema of Effects on Inflation

past history of y itself may "rob" x of any predictive power over y. By concentrating on a variable's ability to explain changes in trend or movements relative to the trend of another variable, the Granger technique can avoid spurious identification of causal relations among variables. In the next section, these tests are performed between money supply variables and a wide number of variables sometimes thought to be indicators of inflationary pressure.

4. Results of the Tests

Granger causality tests between a variable x and a variable y can be performed by estimating equations of form similar to that in (1) for y regressed on lagged x and lagged y, and for x regressed on lagged x and lagged y. If in the former regression lagged values of x have significant effects, x is said to Granger cause y. If in the latter regression lagged y values have significant effects, y is said to Granger cause x. When causality occurs in both directions between the two variables, feedback is said to exist between them.

The tests performed for this study estimated these types of equations using quarterly data for the period beginning in 1957 and ending in 1979. The money supply indicators were percentage growth rates in the monetary aggregates M1 and M2, as defined by the Federal Reserve Board prior to February 1980, and the monetary base, both that as defined by the Federal Reserve Board and that as defined by the Federal Reserve Bank of St. Louis (the latter is adjusted for changes in reserve requirements).

Inflation indicators were percentage rates of change in the Consumer Price Index, total and for nonfood items; in consumer food prices and wholesale farm prices (grouped under "food prices"); in the Wholesale Price Index, total and for nonfarm goods; in wholesale metals and wholesale steel prices ("Industrial Metals"); in wholesale fuel and wholesale petroleum prices ("Fuel Prices"); in nonagricultural and in manufacturing wages; in unit labor costs for private business, for manufacturing, and for nonfarm businesses; in unemployment rates for all workers and for prime age males; and in the GNP Deflator, total and for personal consumption expenditures. Other indicators used as measures of possible inflationary pressure were the government deficit and the percentage rate of change in government spending.

To determine the significance of the various "causal" effects, F-statistics were computed for each equation run. An F-statistic, in this case, measures the significance of the difference of a vector of sample coefficients from the zero vector, much as a t-statistic measures the significance of a single coefficient from zero. The larger an F-statistic, the less likely it is that the true value of the vector is zero. A zero value for a vector of coefficients such as C_1, C_2, ..., C_8 in an equation like (1) would indicate that M_T had no causal effect on P_T. Thus, the significance of the F-statistics in the equations summarized here indicate the significance of the causal effects of the variable used.

The results of these tests are summarized in Table 6.1. Significantly large F-statistics are marked by asterisks, indicating degree of significance. Besides F-statistics, estimates of the long-run "elasticities" (or percent increases in the respective dependent variable elicited by a 1-percent increase in the respective causal variable) are also shown for each equation.[2]

The tests involving consumer prices, wholesale prices, and the GNPD series were performed to determine the nature of the relationship between general inflation indicators and the money supply. Signs of monetary accommodation of these effects would indicate that authorities reacted to accommodate bursts of general inflation. As Table 6.1 indicates, most˙ measures of money supply growth showed significant "causal" effects on these indicators, as the economic theory and previous studies' results would predict. However, only for consumer prices was a reverse "causal" effect onto the money supply found, and this was only for the M1 and M2 indicators. Furthermore, recall that monetary accommodation requires a positive reaction of the money supply to the factor in question. If random increases in the price level were causes of inflation through accommodation, the money supply should increase in response to such price increases. In fact, however, the equations had coefficients for consumer price inflation that varied in sign, that were negative at short lags, and that never showed a significantly positive cumulative effect. If anything, these equations suggested that the Federal Reserve reacts to counter rather than to accommodate CPI inflation. Thus, there was very little sign of monetary accommodation of general inflation pressure.

There was even less sign of accommodation of food prices. These tests would determine whether bad crops or herd cutbacks might cause inflation by raising prices for such an important item as food. Yet while

---

2. Table 6.1 is adapted from Table 1 in Bazdarich (1980).

the money supply variables had a very significant inflationary impact on food prices, no significant reverse effects were found.

For industrial metals prices, significant effects of money growth on these prices were generally found, but reverse effects were found only on the M2 indicator. These again did not have a significantly positive cumulative effect. Significant effects of money on fuel prices were found, but no reverse effects were forthcoming. Therefore, there was little sign of accommodation even of such strategic commodities as metals and fuels.

The most prominent cost-push inflation theory is the idea that wage increases increase costs, force the Fed to accommodate in order to avoid unemployment, and so ultimately cause inflation through a continuing wage-price spiral. Yet as shown in Table 6.1, money supply growth showed very significant inflationary effects on both wages and unit labor costs, but there was absolutely no sign of accommodation of these labor cost variables by the money supply. Even if one were to argue that labor costs cause inflation by increasing unemployment, which is then reacted to by the Fed, the evidence summarized in the table found significant effects of money supply growth on unemployment, but no reverse effect, again belying the wage-push hypothesis.

The last results shown in Table 6.1 pertain to the theory that government deficits or excessive government spending cause inflation. Even in these cases, monetary accommodation is necessary for government fiscal policy to cause inflation. Increased government spending that is financed by taxation merely shifts spending from private to public sources and so needn't be inflationary. Similarly, it is not theoretically clear that a government deficit financed by bond issues increases aggregate demand, since the current bond issues imply higher taxes levied in the future, which might then reduce current private demand analogously to the way current taxation does.[3] Even if bond issues do increase private demand, it should be clear that these are not as inflationary as a government deficit monetized by the Fed. Therefore, this monetization can be asserted to be necessary for government spending to be inflationary.

The Granger causality results for government spending and deficits were rather mixed. For one thing, in contrast to the other indicators of

_____

3. This point was first suggested by David Ricardo, some 200 years ago, and was recently formalized in Barro (1974).

TABLE 6.1

Causality Results Between Various Economic Indicators and the Monetary Aggregates Eight Lags for all Variables, 1959-II to 1979-II[a]

	M1				M2				St. Louis Base				Source Base			
	F¹	LR²	F¹	LR²	F¹	LR²	F¹	LR²	F¹	LR²	F¹	LR²	F¹	LR²	F¹	LR²
Consumer Prices																
All Items	2.9***	1.6	2.6**	0.1	2.1**	1.4	2.4**	0.4	1.7*	1.1	0.9	0.1	2.2**	0.9	1.2	0.0
Food	2.6**	1.9	1.6	-0.1	2.2**	1.5	1.6	0.2	2.4**	1.2	1.0	-0.1	1.5	0.9	1.1	0.0
Excluding food	1.7	1.7	3.3***	0.3	1.2	1.7	1.5	0.4	1.8*	1.2	0.9	-0.2	2.1**	0.9	1.3	-0.2
Wholesale Prices																
All Items	2.8***	2.3	0.6	-0.3	2.2**	1.9	0.9	0.2	1.1	1.5	0.3	0.0	2.2**	1.1	0.8	-0.2
Non-Farm	1.9*	2.2	0.8	-0.1	1.6	1.9	1.5	0.2	0.9	1.4	0.4	0.0	3.0***	1.2	0.7	-0.4
Farm	2.4**	2.4	0.5	-0.4	1.5	2.0	0.7	0.1	1.4	1.5	0.3	0.0	1.8*	0.9	0.7	0.1
Metals	2.4**	2.4	0.9	-0.1	1.4	1.9	2.3**	0.1	1.9*	1.5	1.6	0.0	2.5**	1.4	0.7	-0.5
Steel	1.2	2.4	1.6	0.1	1.0	1.7	2.8**	0.1	1.5	1.6	0.9	0.0	2.0*	1.4	0.6	-0.5
Fuel	2.3**	3.8	0.7	0.0	1.6	3.1	1.0	0.1	1.9*	2.7	0.7	0.1	1.7	2.7	0.9	-0.2
Petroleum	2.1**	3.1	0.8	-0.1	1.1	2.0	1.0	0.1	1.1	1.9	0.4	0.1	1.4	1.9	0.6	-0.4
Wages for Nonagricultural Workers[3]	2.5**	0.5	0.7	0.4	2.4**	0.4	0.6	0.2	3.8***	0.5	1.0	0.7	3.9***	-1.4	0.7	0.5
Manufacturing	1.2	1.5	0.7	0.5	2.3**	1.5	1.1	0.5	3.9***	1.1	0.9	0.1	3.7***	1.1	1.0	0.2
Unit Labor Costs																
Private Business	2.7**	1.6	0.8	0.3	1.7	1.3	1.0	0.5	1.4	1.1	0.7	0.3	2.4**	.10	0.2	-0.7
Manufacturing	1.7	1.6	0.4	0.1	1.4	1.1	0.8	0.2	1.3	0.8	0.9	0.1	1.8*	0.9	0.6	-0.7
Non-farm	2.7**	1.6	0.4	0.3	1.7	1.3	0.7	0.4	1.8*	1.1	0.9	0.2	2.0*	0.9	0.3	-0.7
Unemployment Rates																
All Workers[4]	3.2***	1.3	0.6	0.2	1.4	-0.3	1.2	0.2	1.5	0.6	1.9	0.3	0.8	0.4	0.4	0.1
Males 25-44[4]	3.5***	0.7	0.4	0.0	2.1**	-0.7	1.3	0.1	1.8*	-0.2	0.9	0.2	0.2	0.0	0.8	-0.1

Implicit Deflators

GNP	3.2***	1.3	1.1	0.5	2.3**	1.1	1.1	0.6	2.7**	1.0	1.0	0.4	1.6	0.9	2.0*	-0.6
Personal Consumptions Expenditures	2.4**	1.3	1.0	0.4	2.6**	1.2	1.2	0.5	1.7	1.0	0.8	0.3	2.2**	0.8	0.9	-1.0
Government Deficit[5]	1.7*	5.0	2.3**	0.1	0.5	2.2	1.8*	0.2	0.7	16.6	1.2	0.1	1.8*	15.0	2.0*	0.1
Deficit/GNP Ratio[4,6]	0.8	0.1	0.6	0.4	1.1	0.4	0.6	0.2	0.7	0.8	0.6	0.1	1.1	0.7	1.1	0.5
Government Spending[6]	0.8	0.7	1.4	0.1	0.5	0.6	2.5**	0.2	1.0	0.7	0.7	-0.2	1.0	0.7	0.9	0.4

a   First column of each set shows F-statistic for effect of respective monetary aggregate on "cost" variable: second column shows long-run effect for this relation: third column shows F-statistic for effect of "cost" variable on respective monetary aggregate: fourth column shows long-run effect for this relation.

*   Significant at 10 percent level.

**   Significant at 5 percent level.

***   Significant at 1 percent level.

1   F-Statistic for hypothesis that explanatory variable has no effect.

2   Long-run effect of a permanent one-percentage-point change in explanatory variable on dependent variables: See Appendix I.

3   Sample period: 1966-II to 1979-II.

4   "Cost" variable is in level form.

5   Level of deficit vs. first difference of money supply.

6   Sample period: 1959-II to 1978-IV.

inflationary pressure, no effect of money supply growth on these government spending indicators is seen, although the meaning of this is unclear. Perhaps the time delays in the government budgeting process precluded seeing the effects within two years. Also, while a significant effect of the deficit on the money supply was seen, inherent econometric problems in the structure of this equation cast severe doubt on the meaningfulness of this result.[4] Finally, in earlier tests, government spending was found to have a significant effect on M1 and M2, but this significance disappeared when subsequent data points were added to the sample. In sum, while the results for the government spending indicators were somewhat more equivocal than those for other variables, there was again little reliable evidence of systematic monetary accommodation of these variables.

For the results as a whole, the consistently significant causal effects of the money supply on all the various cost-inflation indicators, and the almost complete absence of significant accommodative effects of the cost indicators on the money supply, is indeed striking. Although the monetary analysis of inflation is supported by this analysis, there is no sign that any cost-push-type variable can systematically explain U.S. inflation over the last twenty years. Section 6 will relate these results to the controllability of inflation issues. In the meantime, Section 5 considers the explanatory power of the various variables for inflation in two recent inflationary episodes.

5. Some Episodes of Inflation

The results in the previous section detailed the ability — or to put it more aptly, the inability — of cost-push and other types of variables to systematically explain money supply growth, and therefore inflation, over a long period: the last two decades. Now it may have occurred to the reader that the nature of monetary accommodation — of various regimes of monetary authorities, with various political experiences and various perceptions of economic phenomena, reacting to offset the contractionary effects of various supply-side shocks — makes it unsusceptible to the rigid equation forms by which it was tested above. That is, it may be thought that accommodative responses are too evanescent a phenomenon to show up clearly in such equations over a long period,

---

4. See Bazdarich (1980), Section 3, and related footnotes there, for a discussion of these problems. The basic problems concern the questionable theoretical validity of a stable econometric relationship between the deficit and the *rate* of money supply growth.

and that the tests are therefore biased against obtaining these results.

Yet it can be countered that if the existence of accommodative responses cannot be adequately tested by these means, it is probably impossible to find an objective way to test them. Again, every inflation experience has seen increases in virtually all money prices and nominal magnitudes, and it is inevitable that the timing of the responses of various variables will vary from experience to experience. Therefore, we could always find an episode where, say, wages increased before the money supply and prices did, or where any other such combination of events occurred. Whether such evidence represents an entirely random coincidence, or a statistical artifact, or a true accommodative incident by the Fed, however, is impossible to tell from one such observation, especially since the period was probably nonrandomly selected to start with.

In spite of possible conceptual problems with the Granger causality tests, then, we can assert that they — or something very similar to them — represent the most objectively meaningful way to test causal hypotheses. If monetary accommodation of inflationary pressures is not a phenomenon that holds up over an extended period, then it's not that predictable a phenomenon in the first place, and not too useful for controlling inflation. Furthermore, given the evolution over time of the economy's response to inflationary money growth, we might also have suspected that the effects of money growth on various inflation indicators would be hard to pick up in formal equations estimated over a long period. Yet these results registered very significantly in the tests. If accommodation has been an important cause of inflation, why didn't it register?

Thus, it can be argued that individual, brief episodes are not very useful for determining the causes of inflation. However, they do provide an interesting check of how universally applicable the long-period results in Section 4 are. Therefore, the rest of this section examines two recent examples of acceleration in U.S. inflation to get some impression of the predictive power of the money supply in this period.

As Figure 6.4 indicates, U.S. CPI inflation rose to about 12 percent in 1974 and stayed at historically high levels throughout the years 1973-1975. Some have attributed this to the OPEC oil embargo and subsequent huge oil price increases, others to worldwide crop failures in 1973, and still others to the sharp worldwide money supply growth in 1971-1973 and dismantling of price controls in mid-1973. This last idea

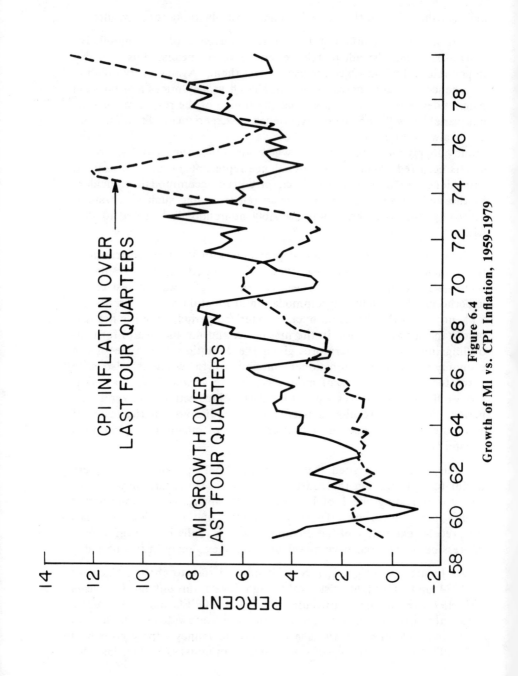

Figure 6.4
Growth of M1 vs. CPI Inflation, 1959-1979

was that the controls artificially suppressed inflation in 1971-1973, but that their removal then unleashed it onto 1973-1975, so that inflation in those years was higher than it would have been if the controls had never been imposed.

The explanatory power of the money supply over a range of inflationary variables has already been seen over a long period of time. Can it explain inflation in such a volatile period as this?

To determine this, an estimated version of the equation (1) was simulated over the period starting in third quarter 1971, the quarter the controls were imposed, through fourth quarter 1975, two years after the controls were fully removed, and thus long enough for their effects to have washed out of the economy. The hypothesis was that if controls merely transferred inflation from one subperiod (1971-1973) to another (1973-1975), the total actual inflation occurring in the period should be little different from that predicted by the money supply over that period, provided such inflation can be reasonably explained by the money supply alone.

Table 6.2 shows the results of simulations of price-money equations for four inflation indicators as explained by M1 from three different sample periods.[5] Recall that the equations discussed in Section 4 were estimated with 1957-1979 data, which includes the present simulation period. To obtain a less biased simulation, equations estimated from periods not including 1971-1975 were also simulated, and these results are shown in Table 6.2 as well. As the table shows, the money supply (M1), alone, in its various simulations, is able to explain virtually the entire retail price inflation occurring in this period.

In contrast, wholesale price inflation is predicted less well, yet this is to be expected when we consider the huge concurrent change in the relative price of oil, which should change the terms of trade between energy and other productive inputs. As a relative price change, this shouldn't — and apparently didn't — have much effect on prices of goods using a wide range of inputs — i.e., retail prices — but it should affect the prices of goods heavily intensive in primary products — i.e., wholesale prices. This was indeed the case.

---

5. Simulations involving the other three money supply indicators (M2, the St. Louis base, and the Federal Reserve Source Base) were also performed, with similar results, and are described in Bazdarich (1980, Section 5).

Table 6.2

Simulation of Price-M1 Equation,
1971-III to 1975-IV

	Sample Period 1959-I to 1971-II		
	Actual Inflation	Simulation Prediction	Simulation Error
Consumer Price Index	36.9%	29.2%	5.9%
Wholesale Price Index	56.2	19.3	31.0
GNP Deflator	35.9	38.2	−1.6
Deflator for personal consumption expenditures	34.3	26.6	6.1
	Sample Period 1959-I to 1971-II, 1976-I to 1979-IV		
CPI	36.9%	38.8%	−1.4%
WPI	56.2	34.5	16.1
GNP Deflator	35.9	33.8	1.6
Personal Consumption Deflator	34.4	32.4	1.5
	Sample Period 1959-I to 1979-IV		
CPI	36.9%	38.5%	−1.2%
WPI	56.2	44.8	7.9
GNP Deflator	35.9	35.6	.3
Personal Consumption Deflator	34.3	33.2	.9

In sum, while the oil and food price shocks in 1973 doubtlessly changed the nature of inflation and other economic developments in 1973-1975, they do not appear to have had much impact on the overall magnitude of what is apparently an otherwise monetary inflation exacerbated by the removal of domestic price controls.

The next period to be considered is 1978-1980. Here also, CPI inflation rose to double-digit levels in 1979 and in 1980. In the early parts of this inflation, many commentators blamed it entirely on excessive wage increases, even though the money supply began to accelerate in 1976, a good two years before inflation reached high levels, and a good year or two before wages accelerated. Also, in the later parts, inflation was blamed on oil price increases in 1979, again despite three previous years of high money growth, and one previous year of very high inflation.

Here again the explanatory power of the money supply over inflation can be described by simulating the price-money equations. Since no general price controls — or their removal — are involved in this period, year-by-year simulations can be meaningfully compared to actual inflation in these years. These simulations were performed — again for equations estimated from samples outside the simulation period — and these are compared to actual inflation and contemporary inflation forecasts in Table 6.3. The CPI and GNPD were simulated here since these two indexes are widely forecasted by major analysts.

Table 6.3 also show inflation forecasts over comparable time periods by several major forecasters. Their inclusion alongside money-price simulations should not be intended as a comparison of forecasting techniques, since the simulations used actual money supply growth over the simulation period, which was unavailable to the forecaster. Rather, the other forecasts are included in order to put simulations errors in the context of forecasting errors by other parties using existing information and state-of-the-art technology.

As Table 6.3 shows, the simulations correctly predict the experienced acceleration in CPI and GNPD inflation, from 6 percent and 5.5 percent respectively in 1977. The simulations are sometimes substantially below actual inflation levels, but they nevertheless compare quite favorably with the forecasts shown for these periods, even though these forecasters used a wide range of information not directly incorporated in the simulation equations. The latter used only current and past money supply information and past price information, and the only

Table 6.3. Simulations of Price-M1 Equation Over
1978-1980 Period and Comparison to Forecasts by Major Analysis

	CPI				GNP Deflator			
	1978	1979	1980	1981	1978	1979	1980	1981
Forecasts by Wharton Econometrics								
12/31/77	5.5	6.3			5.6	5.7		
12/1/78		7.1	6.3			6.6	6.1	
12/3/79			11.3	8.7			9.4	7.8
Data Resources Inc								
12/21/77	5.8	5.3	5.7		6.0	5.4	6.1	
12/27/78		7.8	6.9	6.8		7.4	7.1	6.9
12/20/79			10.4	9.1			9.4	9.2
Time Magazine Bd of Econ								
12/19/77	6.2							
12/25/78		7.5						
12/31/79			9.1(?)[a]					
Simulation Results over Sample period								
1959-II to 1977-IV	7.0	8.0			6.5	7.7		
1959-II to 1978-IV		9.0	8.1			8.8	8.3	
1959-II to 1979-IV			11.8	7.9			8.8	7.2
Actual	9.0	13.3	12.4		8.5	8.1	9.8	

[a] The wording of this forecast makes it unclear whether this rate is for all of 1980 or just the monthly increase in December.

information it offered that was unavailable to the forecasters was actual money supply growth in the simulation periods through 1979.

As with the 1973-1975 period, then, the 1978-1980 inflation experience suggests that the money supply alone can do a creditable job of explaining inflation trends. Although nonmonetary factors certainly had an impact on inflation in the latter period, the money supply is nevertheless able to explain the bulk of inflation in these years. Furthermore, judging from the forecasters, what inflation is left over does not appear to be susceptible to systematic prediction even by very sophisticated economic analysis.

6. Conclusion — Controlling Inflation

If we were to examine Figure 6.4 in the context of the results summarized in Table 6.1, probably the most striking conclusion would be that while growth in the money supply can satisfactorily explain the secular acceleration in inflation shown in Figure 6.4, none of the variables used can explain the coincident secular acceleration in money supply growth. Section 4's results suggest that this has not been a systematic response to pressures from labor markets or unions, energy price trends, food price developments, or other supply-side phenomenan. Also, the evidence systematically linking this acceleration to mounting government spending and deficits is at best tenuous.

Rather, the most accurate description of the underlying forces that have led to continued money supply growth would probably be that they are an amorphous blend of sociological and political pressures. At times they have perhaps manifested themselves in wage demands or industrial pricing practices, at times in government spending propensities, and at times in attempts by central bankers to achieve artificially low interest rates. At all times, they have worked through these channels unsystematically, but in each instance they have become translated into faster money supply growth, apparently in an attempt to monetize away the economy's problems.

This curious structure, of elusive, difficult-to-certify underlying causes of inflation, acting through a remarkably constant monetary channel, has profound implications for policies designed to control inflation. It suggests first that any credible, serious anti-inflation effort must put primary emphasis on controlling and continuing to control money supply growth. No matter what happens to the ignition, the inflationary engine cannot run without fuel.

Second, it suggests that policies designed to control nonmonetary forces are of questionable value. For if no one factor has had a systematic, continuing impact on inflation, controls on any one factor will leave the others free to increase, while controls on the whole economy would stultify economic activity and merely suppress — not remove — the underlying forces at work. Furthermore, it is possible that implementation of such other policies would divert attention from monetary restraint and/or be used as a crutch to control inflation while abandoning monetary restraint — as happened in 1971-1973 — which makes the policies even more disruptive and ultimately ineffective. Finally, if indeed sociological-political pressures/proclivities are the underlying cause of inflation, policies designed to regulate away the effects of these pressures are likely to defeat their own purpose by centralizing decisions and power, thus making them more accessible to manipulation by sociological-political sources.

The conclusion reached from all this analysis is that control of the money supply is the one sure way to control inflation. The evidence is to date not forthcoming that would allow objective identification of more basic causes of inflation, and so other policies are of unlikely or secondary utility. Monetary control, and thus a steadfast refusal to accomodate shocks, will not deliver a quick, easy, or painless elimination of inflation, but it is apparently the only alternative.

References

Barro, Robert J. 1974. "Are Government Bonds Net Wealth?" *Journal of Political Economy* (November), pp. 1095-1117.

Bazdarich, M. J. 1980. "Money, Inflation and Causality in the United States, 1959-1979: Is There a Wage-Price Spiral?" *Federal Reserve Bank of San Francisco Economic Review* (Spring), pp. 50-70.

Friedman, Milton, ed. 1956. *Studies in the Quantity Theory of Money.* Chicago: University of Chicago Press.

Granger, Clive W. J. 1964. *Spectral Analysis of Economic Time Series.* Princeton: Princeton University Press.

Meiselman, David, ed. 1970. *Varieties of Monetary Experience.* Chicago: University of Chicago Press.

Patinkin, Don. 1963. *Money, Interest, and Prices*, 2nd ed. New York: Harper and Row.

Sims, Christopher A. 1972. "Money, Income and Causality." *American Economic Review*, pp. 540-553.

Index

absolute and relative price changes, 1, 15, 20, 23, 134, 169, 171, 185
accomodative money supply, 7, 171, 172, 179
adaptive forecasts and learning, 34, 39, 40
adjustment to inflation, 135, 136
aggregate demand, 22
anchoring, 26, 40
ARIMA processes, 35, 36, 37
autoregressive processes, 35, 36

balance of payments, 115, 122, 123
banks, Federal Reserve, 116, 119, 120, 123, 177
bias
      correcting, 85
      in measuring inflation, 5, 52, 85
      in predicting inflation, 23, 27, 41, 43
bills, treasury, 41
bisquare weights, 65
Bureau of Economic Analysis, 3
Bureau of Labor Statistics, 3, 51, 78, 84

capital stock, effect from inflation, 148
causality, 22, 168
      spurious identification, 168, 169, 172, 177
      test 10, 172ff
causes of inflation, 116, 117, 168ff
Consumer Price Index, 2, 4, 15, 51ff, 177, 183
consumption, effect from inflation, 22, 23, 148
controlling inflation, 9, 167ff
correlation, spurious, 168, 169, 172
cost of living index, 73
cost push, 169, 172, 179, 182

deficit, government, 10, 177, 179
demand, aggregate, 22
distribution of price changes, 23

distribution of price perceptions, 25
drift in inflation rate, 38

efficient markets hypothesis, 28ff
equilibrium
      general, 169
      partial, 119
errors in variables, 54
exchange rate, 117
expectations, rational, 28, 41, 43
expected rate of inflation, 44
      differences among people, 25, 44
      of households, 25
      influences of, 30

farm prices, 177
Federal Housing Administration, 66
Federal Reserve System, 116, 119, 120, 177
      accomodative money suply, 7, 171, 172, 179
      reaction function, 120, 123
fiscal policy, 10, 177, 179
food prices, 177, 183, 187
forecasts
      adoptive, 34, 39, 40
      bias in, 27, 41, 43
      Livingston, 38, 41
      time series, 32, 35, 41, 42
      skewness, 23
      variance in, 27, 31, 189

general equilibrium, 169
government purchased goods and services, 59
Granger causality tests, 10, 169, 172ff, 177, 183
Gross National Product Implicit Deflator, 2, 3, 4, 53, 70, 178
growth, effect from inflation, 148

housing treatment in the CPI, 66
Hume, David, 170

international economy, 7, 115
index, cost of living, 73

learning, adaptive, 34, 39, 40
Livingston surveys of inflation expectations, 27, 41
        bias, 43
        time series analysis, 38

marginal tax rates
        see taxes
markets, efficient, 28ff
moonlight economy, 61
money
        accomodative supply, 7, 171, 172, 179
        aggregates M1 and M2, 177
        demand and supply, 115, 116, 119, 123
        growth, 171, 189
moving average process, 36, 37

new goods measurement problem, 60, 85
noise and signal, equivalent, 5, 55
nominal variables, 168
nonmonetary prices, 85

oil prices, 119, 171, 177, 185
Organization for Economic Cooperation and Development, 7
Organization of Petroleum Exporting Countries, 117, 123
output, effect from inflation, 148

partial equilibrium, 119
perceptions of inflation, 1, 2, 24, 45
        irrational, 42
predicting inflation,
        see forecasts
prices
        absolute and relative, 1, 15, 20, 23, 134, 169, 171, 185
        controls, 183
        farm, 177
        food, 177, 183, 187
        nonmonetary, 85
        oil, 119, 171, 177, 185
        permanent and transitory shocks, 32, 34, 37, 40, 44
        wages, 168, 177
Producer Price Indexes, 2, 3, 4
proximate determinants of inflation, 116, 117

quality change measurement problem, 77

rational expectations, 28, 41, 43
relative and absolute prices, 1, 15, 20, 23, 134, 169, 171, 185
reserve currency country, 117, 122
Ricardo, David, 179

savings, effect from inflation, 9, 140ff
signal to noise ratio, equivalent, 5, 55
social costs of inflation, 151, 162
statistical estimation of inflation, 31, 33
survey evidence on inflation expectations, 24

tax rate, marginal, 9
    calculation of, 158ff
    defined, 135
    effect from inflation, 136, 137
    importance of, 136ff
    response of savings, 140ff
terms of trade, 115, 117, 123
treasury bills market, 41
time series analysis,
    causality testing, 10, 169, 172ff, 177, 183
    of inflation, 32, 35, 41, 42
    lagged relationships, 172
    of Livingston forecasts, 38, 41

underlying rate of inflation, 33, 38, 39
unemployment, 10, 43, 171
unexpected inflation, 21, 43, 134, 135
United States inflation history, 6, 15

variability
    of forecasts, 27, 31, 189
    of inflation, 18, 22
    of relative prices, 21

wages, 168, 177
wage push, 168, 171, 172
wars, effect on inflation, 77, 123
Wholesale Price Index, 81

About the Editor

William A. Gale is a member of the Technical Staff, Statistics and Data Analysis Research Department, Bell Telephone Laboratories. After earning his Ph.D. in physics from Rice University, he worked at Bellcomm in Washington, D.C., in support of the manned space flight program. After moving to Bell Laboratories following the closing of Bellcomm, he studied the demand for long-distance telecommunication. Studying the limits of accuracy of demand analyses led to research on the measurement of price changes, which in turn led to an interest in inflation. As a result, he is currently researching the effects of inflation and the pricing of congestible resources. Dr. Gale continues to have a wide range of interests; he is the editor of the recently published *Life in the Universe, the Ultimate Limits to Growth.*